FAITH
in the
FAMILY

Also by Dale Salwak

FAITH
in the
FAMILY

honoring and strengthening
home and spirit

DALE SALWAK

NEW WORLD LIBRARY
NOVATO, CALIFORNIA

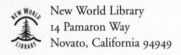

New World Library
14 Pamaron Way
Novato, California 94949

Copyright © 2001 by Dale Salwak
Front cover design by Mary Beth Salmon
Text design and typography by Tona Pearce Myers

Unless otherwise noted, the Scripture quotations contained herein are from the *New Revised Standard Version Bible,* copyright © 1989 by the Division of Christian Education of the National Council of Churches of Christ in the United States of America. All rights reserved. Used by permission.

Library of Congress Cataloging-in-Publication Data
Salwak, Dale.
  Faith in the family : honoring and strengthening home and spirit /
Dale Salwak.
      p. cm.
Includes bibliographical references and index.
  ISBN 1-57731-160-4 (alk. paper)
  1. Family—Religious aspects—Christianity. 2. Salwak, Dale. I. Title.
BV4526.3 .S25 2001
261.8′3585—dc21   00-011658

First Printing, February 2001
ISBN 1-57731-160-4
Printed in Canada on acid-free paper
Distributed to the trade by Publishers Group West

10 9 8 7 6 5 4 3 2 1

For my family

Soli Deo Gloria

CONTENTS

ACKNOWLEDGMENTS

I am grateful to my publishers, particularly Marc Allen and Becky Benenate, who had enough confidence in me and in the idea for this book to commission its writing; and to Dr. Reginald C. Clarke, Laura Nagy, and Rudy Saldaña, along with my parents, Dr. and Mrs. Stanley F. Salwak, and New World Library's editorial director, Georgia Hughes, for reading and helping me to refine the manuscript: Their gifts of conversation and critique are of inestimable value.

I also remain indebted beyond easy measure to all those who have shared their lives, their struggles, their insights, and their courage, and from whom I have learned so much of what is in this book. In some instances, to ensure the privacy of the families that I interviewed and to protect their anonymity, while preserving their stories, names and other identifying details have been changed.

Finally, I give thanks for the blessings of a loving, supportive family: my wife, Patti, and my son, Ryan. Without them, and without my own parents and grandparents along with my brother, Glenn, and his family, I could never have written this book. It is to them all that I append the dedication (to borrow from Johann Sebastian Bach): Glory to God Alone.

We were wise indeed, could we discern
truly the signs of our time;
and by knowledge of its wants and advantages,
wisely adjust our own position in it.

— THOMAS CARLYLE

*E*very generation has worried about the decline of
the family, and ours is no exception. For twenty
years I have mulled over the alarming words of one of my
teaching colleagues who said of modern America (and by
implication, all of modern Western civilization):

> If our families crumble,
>> then we are dead.
> Well, our families are crumbling,
>> and we are dying.

Is this great institution really in trouble? Is our society fundamentally hostile toward the family? And if so, is there hope for a restoration? Only after the experiences and lessons of the two decades since I heard his words have I achieved enough perspective to examine them with at least a modicum of insight and clarity.

To judge from the media, the signs of a breakdown in fundamental relationships are everywhere. Half of all marriages in the United States now end in divorce, the highest rate of any industrial nation in the world. One-third of all households are held together by a single parent, and 42 percent of children of divorced parents haven't seen their fathers for a year or more. There is a surge of drug abuse, of new sexually transmitted diseases including AIDS, of out-of-wedlock pregnancies (in 1963, 6.5 percent; in 1999, 30 percent), of domestic violence, and of abortions (now over one million a year). Thousands of children today are confronted by broken homes only to end up, says James Q. Wilson, "on the mean streets of America with no fathers, crack-abusing mothers, and drug dealers as role models." A greater number of teenagers and young adults in America die from suicide than from cancer, AIDS, birth defects, influenza, heart disease, stroke, and pneumonia *combined.* Runaways number one million a year.

In every community, class, and age group, it seems, is a growing disrespect for parents and other authorities, a lowering of standards of decency, and an increasing rebelliousness among youths — many of whom are isolated, self-centered, tolerant of everything and committed to nothing. Recent school shootings, in which teenaged boys have gunned down fellow students and even teachers before killing themselves, have already become a national icon for the disconnection, despair, and disaffection many youths feel and some express through acts of senseless, explosive violence.

We live in a time, philosophers tell us, when civilization is shifting its basic outlook — a major turning point in history when the presuppositions on which society is structured are being "analyzed, sharply challenged, and profoundly changed." Why?

Some blame technology and the endlessly diverting electronic advances of a popular, consumer-driven culture that assaults the privacy of the home, interferes with relationships, and devalues life. Others accuse a corrosive legal system that has bit by bit undermined parental authority, weakened school discipline, and obstructed moral education. Lawsuits and judicial decisions, for example, have barred organized prayer in public schools, forbidden the posting of the Ten Commandments, and prohibited the mention of God in the classroom.

Still others point to the news media and the entertainment industry that transmit "counterculture values" of drug- and alcohol-induced escapism, cultic obsession, wanton sex, and glorified violence. And others attribute the decline to the cumulative results of the "revolution" on American campuses in the 1960s ("Down with the Establishment!" "Make Love, Not War!" "If It Feels Good,

Do It!") and the 1973 U.S. Supreme Court decision on abortion (*Roe* v. *Wade*). All of this, say numerous commentators, has led to an epidemic of depression, suicide, and personal emptiness — along with an inability to sustain deep and enduring personal relationships.

But as I argue in the pages that follow, these trends (and others) are merely the symptoms of something deeper and more insidious. The core of the problem as I see it is a spiritual one, and therefore the solution is spiritual as well.

Not long ago over dinner in our home, the Reverend Shuma Chakravarty, pastor of the First Parish Church in Dorchester, Massachusetts, and a close friend of the late Mother Teresa, related to me the story of how they met.

One day, when Shuma was only twelve years old and living with her family in Calcutta, Mother Teresa visited her home to collect a painting that Shuma's brother had made and wished to donate to an orphanage. Upon seeing the diminutive nun for the first time, Shuma exclaimed: "Your face is so shiny! When I grow up I want to be just like you!"

The adults in the room, quite embarrassed for the guest, tried to quiet the child. But Mother Teresa was not embarrassed: She approached Shuma, lowered herself to one knee; took hold gently of Shuma's tiny chin with her large, strong hands; looked deeply into her eager eyes; and asked:

> Can you love? Can you really love — until it hurts?
> Can you give? Can you really give — without
>   counting the cost?

These two searching questions, coming from the heart of a woman of unshakable faith and total surrender to the Word, forever changed Shuma. They guided her as a calling for her own life; and much later as a student at Boston College and Harvard, and now as a pastor, she has returned to them often, seeking to understand their implications for both herself and her ministry.

The questions asked of Shuma are also ones that we must ask of ourselves if we are to discover the nature of our own spirituality. And it is only through that discovery that we become able to relate to others in a healthy, caring, and selfless manner.

Jesus told us that one of the greatest commands is to love others as we love ourselves; the single institution that enables us to do so is the family, for it is there that we form and strengthen our visions of ourselves and at the same time learn to support, understand, and nurture others.

The family is both a looking glass and a pillar, giving us at once the best chance to see ourselves clearly and to receive the love and affirmation we need to survive in a dangerous world. Strength in the family leads to strength in the spirit, and a strong spirit engenders a strong family. The two cannot be disconnected without injury to both. Likewise, healing one leads to healing in the other.

On another occasion Mother Teresa observed that the greatest disease in the West today is not tuberculosis or leprosy or AIDS, but being unwanted, unloved, and uncared for. "We can cure physical diseases with medicine," she said, "but the only cure for loneliness, despair, and hope-lessness is love. There are many in the world who are dying for a piece of bread but there are many more who are dying for a little love. The poverty in the West is a different type of poverty — it is not only a poverty of loneliness but also of spirituality. There's a hunger for love, as there is a hunger for God."

As a part-autobiographical, part-historical meditation on the importance of staying connected to and maintain-ing a spiritual center in one's life, *Faith in the Family* is both a celebration of the family as it can and ought to be, and a gentle but unsentimental inquiry into the contemporary problems (as well as some solutions) facing our society.

While I explore my personal observations and memories along with the stories of many others, I hope readers will be encouraged to confront the truth of their own families' inner lives and to understand that no institution is more worth fighting (and praying) for. "If you want to save the empire," Confucius affirmed, "you must first save the family."

One final word: I need to apply what follows as much as anyone. Although I include in my portraits the ideal, it is an ideal for which I still yearn, and will continue to do so for the rest of my life. By writing this book, I am min-istering to myself as much as to anybody. In the wisdom of the fifth-century monastics known as the Desert Fathers, may I be converted by my own words.

— DALE SALWAK, AUGUST 2000

the need for connections

*To be rooted is perhaps the most important
and the least recognized need of the human soul.*

— SIMONE WEIL

On a return trip to my hometown of Amherst,
Massachusetts, after a thirty-five-year absence, I
stood on my street, before the house my father had built,
and thought: What if suddenly I could not remember
where I was born or where I had lived as a child? What
if I had forgotten my father's name, or my mother's, or
my brother's, or my grandparents' and aunts' and uncles'
and cousins' names? Would I be the same person? No:

1

Because I wouldn't have a story to tell. For story is part of my soul, and I would have lost part of my soul.

Although "most of us know the parents or grandparents we come from, we go back much further," says V. S. Naipaul in *A Way in the World*. "We go all of us to the very beginning; in our blood and bone and brain we carry the memories of thousands of beings." Of this essayist Michel de Montaigne wrote in the sixteenth century: "What a wonderful thing it is that that drop of seed from which we are produced bears in itself the impressions, not only of the bodily shape, but of the thoughts and inclinations of our fathers!"

Yet that secure sense of personal history is not a given in all families. Indeed, some children grow up unaware of the long invisible thread binding them to others, while many others grow up merely unappreciative. A few, sadly, have good reason to reject their family ties altogether, leaving an inner hole that is difficult to fill up, even over a lifetime.

How blessed I feel, then, when I say that my own parents and grandparents are so deeply a part of me that I can't even conceive of life without them. I grew up in a good home, in an atmosphere of confidence and harmony, surrounded by people who had a sound sense of what is worthwhile in life, who didn't just talk about the moral and religious life, but practiced it.

Within me to this day are resonances of the loving,

vibrant, affirming, reassuring voices of my parents — two of the most moral people I have ever known. My brother and I carried from our childhood the certainty that there was nothing that they would deny us — if we *needed* it. Somehow we knew that in their spirits was always the desire for our own well-being, and when we had success, they cheered inside themselves without even having to summon it up or create it.

I am convinced that without their gentle but consistent prodding and entire devotion neither my brother nor I would be where we are today in our respective careers and personal lives. Our parents and grandparents have been at the heart of everything we have done. They taught us to believe in ourselves. And they made it possible for us to pass their legacy of love along to our own families, with the hope that our children's children will feel the touch of ancestors unseen but ever present in spirit.

For us, as I'm sure for many others, possessions help keep a person's memory alive: This rocker was grandmother's, that cornet was left by grandfather. Each year as Christmas fast approaches, however, a certain photograph haunts me and captures my imagination.

The house at 93 Walnut Hill was a large one even by

present standards; to a child it seemed less like a house than a city. My Christmas Eve memories are the product of steep stairs, lamp-lit rooms, upstairs whispers, closets explored in solitude, distant noises of creaking floors and gurgling pipes, and the sounds of a gentle wind under the tiles.

My maternal grandfather, Frank Bachelder, always dressed in much the same way: a dark blue cardigan, unbuttoned; trousers of thickish gray flannel; an open-necked white shirt; black walking shoes; a visor pulled down over his forehead. I rarely saw him without a cigar, and I grew to love the aroma. My grandmother, Gertrude, a stout confident woman approaching eighty in my remembered image, wore a patterned blue dress, gray sweater, and low-heeled shoes buckled across the top. My grandparents were true New Englanders, sentimental and traditional, wise and utterly honest, easily moved both to irony and to tenderness. She was hard of hearing; he was not.

That Christmas Eve we sat round the kitchen table. Out came the cards and cribbage board, black from years of use. Smudge Face, the ginger-colored cat, sat on a high footstool and watched as if hoping for a wrong move.

"Your deal, Grandpa!" I yelled.

"I'm not deaf!" he said, for perhaps the hundredth time in my life. Often, of course, he just let it ride, depending on how he felt.

"Right, now my play!" I yelled again.

This time he let it ride: Grandma was handing him a

glass of milk and two molasses cookies (called "Monkey cookies") at that moment. Later, each of us — Mom and Dad, my brother Glenn and I, Grandma and Grandpa, Aunt Katie — was allowed to open just one gift.

The bedroom I slept in once belonged to my Aunt Myrtle. It was high ceilinged and very dark; bookshelves stuffed full lined the walls, and a slightly dusty smell was reminiscent of a secondhand bookshop. Pictures of my own making or cut from brightly-colored Christmas catalogs were taped to the walls.

I loved the view from the thinly frosted window. Through the spindly trees I could see the snow on the crest of the hill, sparkling like diamonds; then below it the winding road lined with houses at some points and deserted at others; and here and there a dark and deep patch of woodland, and beyond, the railroad tracks. The sound of a train whistle at night still conjures up those evenings from my boyhood.

How many Christmas Eves had I spent in that bed, intent on my dreamgame, which absorbed the entire landscape: the quiet house, the trees, the snow, the tracks in the distance? I firmly believed that I heard reindeer hooves on the roof. Was that a rustle? A footstep? A whisper?

It is clear that at this time — the all-important formative years of six, seven, and eight — I was living (as C. S. Lewis, my favorite author at the time, wrote) "almost entirely in my imagination; or at least...the imaginative

experience of those years now seems to me more important than anything else." Yet, as did Lewis, I still experience times when there suddenly arise in me "without
warning, and as if from a depth not of years but of centuries," the memories of those Christmas Eves on Walnut
Hill.

And so perhaps you can understand why I had to
return, and why it was hard to leave. So many years had
passed since our family left Amherst for Indiana and,
later, for California. Yet during that summer weekend I
found with little trouble my childhood home and schools,
and, in nearby Orange, the houses and graves of my
grandparents and my Aunt Myrtle, who had recently
passed away and was buried next to her parents in the
cemetery behind the local library. To me these people to
whom I am genetically and spiritually tied will always be
a symbol for everything that is good: hardworking, honest, strong willed, uncomplaining, with a faith that was
the essential underpinning of their lives.

I also located the church of my childhood: the flag-
stone gray First Congregational Church on Main Street in
Amherst, just east of the town square and across the street
from the house where poet Emily Dickinson once lived.

A side door was ajar, so I slipped in, found my way
easily to the sanctuary, which was empty, and sat down
in the sixth-row aisle seat — where as a child I had
many times sat next to my mother — and revisited that

comfortable sensation I'd always had when I was next to her singing hymns, that feeling of being safe.

The silence of the church was itself a sound: low and steady, sheltering and restorative, and I realized in an instant that I had never stopped missing this dimly remembered sanctuary.

Graham Greene wrote that "there is always one moment in childhood when the door opens and lets the future in." For me, I believe that occurred in 1952, when I was five years old and listening to the voice of the pastor as he baptized my brother, Glenn. My mother had written his words down for me, as she did every Sunday, to help me recreate at home what I had experienced in church. As the pastor spoke his blessing, I first felt the tug on my spirit that would eventually grow into my own fully realized faith.

"There's an inner child of the past in all of us," he had said. "And baptism stirs that child, and we remember that we are children of God and belong to Him, and we reach out for the Heavenly Father."

That scene typifies many of the things I have always loved about Massachusetts: its charm, its peacefulness, the way its people embody a certain tenderness for life, but most of all its rich history, its deep culture — backed up by so many years of personal memories. We cannot go home again. But we can return in our hearts, and we can take from home the best of what we have learned and experienced, and build from there.

The last evening of my visit to Amherst I spent at a memorable — and at moments tearful — dinner with Stashya, the widow of one of my uncles. As I drove away the next day I became aware of a powerful longing to turn back the calendar to the 1950s and return with my family to the house on Walnut Hill. It still stands, much as I remembered it. I could see a light shining from behind the front room curtain, but no one was at home.

In my mind and heart, however, someone will always be "at home" there, for that sense of security and acceptance can withstand time far better than can clapboards or bricks and mortar. If we build the emotional foundation of our families on solid ground, then the relationships that frame and finish the structure cannot help but be solid too. The materials are love and nurturance, time and attention, patience and guidance. It is difficult work that sometimes saps our resources and tests our strength, but the end result is well worth it: a family in the true sense of the word, a psychic "place" where a child can safely grow.

While I can always remember "home" with this sense of warmth and welcome, some of my friends have no desire to recall their own childhoods; indeed, if they could, they would erase them from their memories altogether. Such an impulse may avoid pain, but only temporarily.

"From the point of view of the soul, it's not good to let go of the past," Thomas Moore reminds us in *Soul Mates.* "Better to revisit its painful and pleasurable moments, thus keeping ourselves intact, full, and nourished within." However much pain it causes, we must put together the severed pieces or we will forever be hampered in our efforts to get on with the business of living.

Just as I continue to carry the strength imparted to me by a solid family upbringing, those less fortunate individuals carry with them the jumble of emotions that accompany neglected or abused childhoods. And just as I am sustained by the love my parents gave me, they are plagued by the absence of parental love when they needed it most. They may be able to suppress the memories but more insidious is the sense of loss.

I am reminded of Sara (as I'll call her here). We were friends in elementary school, then parted, only to meet again by chance at Purdue University, where we were both English majors. As I became reacquainted with Sara I grew to appreciate her as a confident, bold young woman who seemed to have an unusually clear view of her future. Snapshots from that time reveal her with the sort of gentle, intelligent face we expect to see in wise, kind teachers, reflecting an unselfishness and patient endurance. She had that wonderful combination of quiet charm and good manners that made you feel she really wanted to talk to you. Indeed, there was something about her pale blue eyes, as they looked out from behind her gold, wire-rimmed glasses, that suggested she took in everything she saw.

Beneath that warm exterior, however, I sensed a secret sorrow: the ghosts of regrets, perhaps, or the shadows of some deep longing. Erich Fromm has written wisely that our most basic fear is the threat of being separated from other humans. The first separation from caregivers in infancy, for example, creates fear and sadness in babies and is at the very root of all later anxiety and sorrow in adulthood. I'm certain that this is in part what the English poet William Wordsworth had in mind when he wrote of "the still, sad music of humanity." I now know that it is this feeling of detachment from others that I sensed in Sara.

My intuition was confirmed several years later when she told me how she had awakened one morning to hear herself chanting over and over: "I pray, Lord, that you will watch us. I pray, Lord, that you will protect us." She had been saying the words in a dream in which she and an unidentified child were visiting a prison, apparently waiting, leaning against the wall of a small room. A man, whose face she could not see, entered rather ominously garbed in a dark, ankle-length wool coat. She understood him to be the warden. Suddenly she realized there was a lockdown in the prison because inmates had revolted, and she and the child were trapped in the room with other strangers. Vainly seeking a way out, she went to a window through which she glimpsed a grassy field where a few people stood. When she turned back to the cell itself, everyone seemed to have escaped except the child and herself.

Then the scene switched. Now she was seated at a table, eating; it was the dining room in her childhood home, but the uncomfortable, trapped, and threatened feeling she'd experienced in the prison cell was the same. Other people — including a dark-clad figure to her left and a woman to her right — were waiting for her to do or say something, as if she would be in trouble if she did not speak. Sara felt compelled to ask the woman two questions: "Which is the nurturer? Which is the traitor here?" She spoke softly, almost without moving her lips, so that no one else would hear. She had a powerful feeling that she should be very careful; it was dangerous to say or ask too much. Then she started chanting the words that woke her, "I pray, Lord, that you will watch us. I pray, Lord, that you will protect us."

A year of therapy helped her to identify the figure in the wool coat in the prison cell and the same figure at the dinner table: It was her father. The woman at the table was her mother: passive, submissive. And the feelings of danger, entrapment, and betrayal began to make sense to Sara.

"There is a part of me that has always felt very, very

sad," she confided to me one day after class, "and now I know why. It is a core of sadness that I experience when I realize what is missing from my childhood. All my life I've been yearning for what is out of reach. Here I am, twenty-one years old, and yet there is a part of me that is not whole, that cries out just like a child for the Mommy and Daddy I didn't ever have."

The young child, vulnerable as it is, needs nurturance and protection and looks to the only people it can — its parents — to supply them. When parents are unavailable or unresponsive, the results can be devastating.

"One day through my bedroom window I saw a father holding his daughter's hand," Sara said, "and my heart sank." She had never known the warmth and protection such a simple gesture suggests.

Rather than disappearing as the child matures, this universal and natural need for affinity and affection remains, and can become a festering wound if, as in Sara's case, it is not attended to. In other words, we never outgrow that childhood need if it is unmet in the first place, and the emptiness in our soul allows many destructive emotions to rush in. Sara's dream helped her see that she was full of anger, and when she felt anger, she felt fear, and she wanted to withdraw or escape from that emotional prison. She said she sometimes imagined ending her life, to join the people on the green field beyond the window of her cell. Through that fantasy she could confront the menace and resentment she felt, express her helplessness, and "get even" with her father and avenge his brutal treatment.

"I remember the times he would come into my bedroom, pull off his belt, slam the windows closed so the neighbors wouldn't hear, and begin to hit me across my legs. It was physical pain, but more than that. He was hitting me in anger and frustration. What had I done? Horsed around when I was supposed to be in bed? Talked through the wall with my sister when we should have been asleep? Not done a chore? And Mom was in the background, watching, saying only, 'Allan! That's enough!' And he would yell, 'Jen, stay out of this!'

"Then he would leave, slamming the door, and I'd be left to sob, then rage into my pillow. I wanted to get back at him, but I couldn't."

A child whose need for tenderness is met by cruelty feels not just afraid and confused, but powerless. Parents in healthy families encourage their children to express their emotions in positive ways; they talk *with* their kids rather than merely talking *to* them, and, more important still, they listen. But those lines of communication so vital to a child's emotional development are cut off in toxic family environments like Sara's, and the child is left with a tidal wave of emotions he or she has no means to cope with.

One time, Sara said, she scratched her initials into the bedroom windowsill with a nail file, a kind of silent but lasting rebellion. Often when her father fell ill or injured himself, a part of her smiled while another part felt guilty over the smile. Many times after being punished she would have to sit at the dining room table for dinner, with his terrifying presence not far away.

"I couldn't look my father in the eyes," she said. "I just looked down at my plate, in tears and shame, and tried to eat. And there were few if any words from him: no reassurance, no cuddling, no healing process. Nothing. And just thinking of that now makes me very sad and I wish I could climb into his lap and cry for an hour without fear of belittlement or rejection."

Those feelings of entrapment, betrayal, and frustration followed her until her dream made her begin to confront them.

After graduation in 1969, Sara and I went our separate ways. I moved to California and we corresponded occasionally. In 1979, a year before she died of pneumonia, Sara wrote, "I realized I had suffered a loss but had never grieved that loss. I had to experience the anger, the sadness, the disappointment first, then I could forgive, then I could let go of my anger. 'If I want certainty in my path,' said St. John of the Cross, 'I must walk in darkness.' And so I have.

"God calls us to forgive, meaning to cancel the debt we are owed. I came to a point when I realized I didn't *have* to collect the debt, that God will take care of it. I know I can no longer collect the debt I was owed, so I just wrote it off. I never really reconciled with my father, but that's okay — I understand, and I appreciate, and I've forgiven."

Sara's example, as much as anyone's, has helped me to understand how vital a healthy family environment is to every child, and how pervasive and lasting the effects of bad parenting can be. It has also taught me to value what my own family gave me all the more. Loving and caring parents speed us on our life's journey; they show us what we can and should be.

For all of us are here, in this world, because and only because of our parents, and *their* parents, and *their* parents, as far back as we can trace, and even further. We did nothing to earn our life; we did nothing to deserve it. It is a gift through the marvelous miracle of our parents — and of God.

And that has led me to understand more deeply why I am so ambitious, so driven. And why so much of what I have done in my life has been in the hope of evoking my parents' pride. It is to be worthy. It is to honor them.

Two individuals, two families, two journeys: so different in outcome, in experience. Indeed, loving and giving are what connect us to other human beings, and connection is a need that resides at our deepest core. And the strength and quality of that connection reverberates for better or worse through our own lives and the ties we forge.

to care for the old

In the case of storks the old birds remain in the nests because they are unable to fly, but their children...traverse the whole earth and sea, and from all quarters provide their parents with what is necessary for them....Is it not right, then, after these examples, that men who neglect their parents should cover their faces from shame?

— PHILO

One night when I was fourteen, I was startled awake. The luminous red dial of my bedside clock read 3:15. What had awakened me was the sound of my mother's voice in the room across the hall. It was whispered but audible, and it said, "Stan! Are you breathing?"

Or that's what I thought she said. And a chill of fear, of dread, coursed straight down my back. Suddenly I had an intimation of what I hadn't known before, an awareness I would have from that moment on.

It didn't matter that within thirty seconds my reason told me she had said "dreaming," not "breathing." That moment of illumination (I can call it nothing else) changed me forever, for the fear implicit in that imagined inquiry undermined a certainty that every child assumes: My parents will be there, a constant, no matter what. Suddenly I was aware for the first time that that assumption was not true, and I lost a little bit of my innocence. Once lost, it could not be reclaimed.

Only much later did I see the episode as one of God's gifts, an awakening that allowed me to face a painful but necessary reality: My father would die, one day, as would my mother. Before that moment I had never truly considered that loss. But the revelation opened the way for me to understand that no matter how much we care for our parents, no matter how much we need their affirmation and love, eventually we must gently release them. Albert Schweitzer once wrote, "We must all become familiar with the thought of death if we want to grow into really good people.... Thinking about death produces love for life."

Thirty years later, I was sitting with my pastor in his study, and the scene once again played itself out in my mind.

"May I ask you a question?" I asked suddenly. "You

always seem to have a word that I can hold onto, that helps."

"Of course."

"Sometimes I find myself dwelling on the inevitable death of my parents, and I feel fear, but I don't know why."

"All you can do," he said, "is give thanks for their lives."

Give thanks for their lives. Yes: That's what I have held onto. What a help are those five words with family and friends, indeed anyone to whom we are connected and care about.

For in giving thanks for their lives, we are made aware of the great gifts they have given us: the sacrifices, the support, the good sense, the succor. Little wonder that throughout history, and in most cultures, there has been a lasting reverence for age. Elders have always been respected for their ties to the past and for the hard-earned, accumulated wisdom of a lifetime that they transmit to future generations.

During the golden age of Athenian society (480–399 B.C.), for example, law commanded that sons support their infirm or aged parents; and public opinion enjoined modesty and respect in the behavior of the young toward the old. Plato took it for granted that a well-bred youth would be silent in the presence of his seniors unless asked to speak.

At the height of the Roman Empire (508–262 B.C.), the young never questioned their duty to care for the old. The old remained to the end the first consideration and the last authority; and after their deaths their graves were honored as long as a male descendant survived.

In Judaism, many healthy years are understood to be a blessing granted by God. The fifth commandment — Honor your father and mother — was interpreted to mean that although caring for aged parents may be a burden, it is rewarded by long life for those who fulfill it. One hundred and twenty became the ideal age because Moses had reached that age with his sight "unimpaired and his vigor unabated" (Deut. 34:7). Rabbi Joseph Telushkin reminds us that some Jews continue to open correspondence with the inscription "Dear [addressee], *amush*," a Hebrew acronym for *ad meah v'esrim shana,* "may you live to one hundred and twenty years," and this blessing is frequently offered to people on their birthdays. This reverent and caring attitude toward elders is also affirmed in the fact that virtually every Jewish community maintains some kind of special home for the aged.

Of all the relationships a person will ever have, that between a parent and a child is the most complicated. When a parent dies, we lose several relationships: the affirming, nurturing parent of our childhood; the guardian who tried to mold and discipline us when we were growing up; the friend in our adult years; and if the

parent lives long enough, the dependent, vulnerable elderly person. One friend who had recently lost her mother
wrote to me: "I'm so glad I did what needed to be done,
and said what needed to be said, before she died. I can't
imagine living as so many of my friends do, still with
unfinished business, unresolved conflicts with their
deceased parents."

Perhaps this is why Jewish law decrees that a person
who loses a husband or wife, brother, sister, or child
remains in a state of mourning for thirty days, but
mourns nearly a year for a parent.

In the traditional Japanese family, as well, reaching a
great age is esteemed and with every additional year the
elder is valued even more. I have been to Asia nine times,
but the journey that made the most lasting impression on
me was my first, in 1977, when I stayed for a week with a
family in Osaka. The household was characterized by discipline and order and my hosts were gracious and generous, but what impressed me most was the respect and
loyalty the children showed the elders. A shrine in the
family living room was where they paid homage to the
ancestors. Along with the husband, wife, and two children, the family included the strict but kind maternal
grandmother — eighty-nine then, feeble, and yet still very
much at the moral center of a social unit where she was
respected and listened to. Here I found a sterling example
of what an anonymous Confucian scholar meant when he

said: "Filial piety is what distinguishes men from birds and beasts."

Many families honor the departed with photographs or other displays, with keepsakes and other mementos. I am writing these words with a Parker fountain pen: dark blue casing, gold tip, with a tapered end that is ringed with a gold band. My Aunt Myrtle bought it in 1931, the year she began teaching high school science. She carried it with her into the Women's Army Corps (1942–1946); then to Los Alamos where she participated in the Manhattan Project; then to the University of Chicago where she worked in metal analysis until 1973. This, too, is the very pen she used to write all of her letters, to sign all of our birthday and Christmas cards. I feel a special connection with her every time I pick it up and begin to compose.

Another of my family's prized possessions is a wooden Seth Thomas chime clock that has been handed down from generation to generation and now belongs to my brother. In our grandparents' home, no one had a wristwatch. There wasn't even an alarm clock at each person's bedside. The whole family told time by this clock. It still ticks away the seconds, each movement of the hands serving as a reminder that although our grandparents are gone, their spirits are very much alive.

Such material things revitalize our memories; a table, a favorite teacup, a well-worn hat, or fishing rod can reverberate with reminiscence and love. By paying homage to objects we perpetuate the veneration of those to whom they once belonged — their beliefs, their values, their wisdom, their likes and dislikes: in short, their humanity and its influence on who *we* are.

Children who grow up well nurtured tend to love the old. Perhaps that helps to explain why since our childhood my brother and I have felt most at ease in the company of people older than ourselves — and why, even in childhood, we were aware of the fragility of life. When I shared this recently with my mother, she confirmed that she had felt the same way. Part of the reason is that, like her, we spent so much of our early years with our grandparents who were in their sixties when we came on the scene and lived into their early nineties. Both my mother and father were very close to their parents. When they talked about going to see them, they always talked about going "home." Now I know that feeling.

Including children in our dealings with our elders is important in many ways. Family gatherings and activities — Sunday dinners, holiday gatherings, summer picnics, quiet conversations on the front porch — can provide our children with some of their happiest memories. Kids love to hear the stories that are inevitably told at such times, and they learn about family and social history, significant personal events, and norms both lasting and changing. In addition, as children watch the respect and honor shown their elders by family and friends, they have models to follow for interactions with their own children and their own parents later on: An honored parent and, possibly, grandparent are what we can hope to become.

In 1960, when our family moved from Massachusetts to Indiana, I could sense in my mother a reluctance to leave her parents, who were by then well into their eighties. Wisely, they reassured her: "Don't worry about us. Your place is with your family. We'll be fine." And then quoting Isaiah, her mother added, and "even to your old age I am He, and to gray hairs I will carry you" (46:4, RSV).

And so we moved. But my mother did worry: How could she not? Without fail over the next nine years, she wrote them a letter every day just as she had written to my father during the war. On four occasions she and her sister, Myrtle, flew back to Massachusetts after their father called to say they needed help.

I remember when my grandmother died: July 18, 1969, the same weekend as Ted Kennedy's Chappaquidick accident and the Apollo moon landing. The week before, my mother and her sister had stayed with my grandmother in the nursing home, then returned home. To this day my mother remembers my grandmother's last spoken words: "Well, if I don't see you again, you'll know it's as it should be."

That evening, the sun had gone down, a chill set in, and then came the call. Mom left the next day. After she returned a week later, I don't remember her talking much about what must have been an enormous burden at the time. That is part of the New England reserve: You just did what you had to do, sadly but without complaining and certainly without resentment. But there was also genuine relief. No longer need she worry. Her mother was safe, "in the loving hands of God," to be joined, as she learned two years later, by her father on November 11 (Armistice Day). Such respect and love for her own aging parents taught me a lot.

For the day will come when the parents who nurtured us will be the ones who need nurturing. I feel a warm glow of gratitude that I am in a position where I can help my own parents. Once after a particularly difficult week, my father said to me, "I'm sorry I have to put you through all this. You have a life to lead, I know." To which I responded, without hesitation, "Nonsense. It's a privilege to help." The last years of a relationship are important ones; my mother and father, through loving care of their own parents, taught me that lesson.

One day I asked my mother how her own situation as a senior citizen compared to that of her parents. "To me," she said, "it's like a movie being played over, and your father and I are the lead characters." We could do worse than to observe, listen, and learn.

I was able to play such a loving role when my father had surgery, and it was fulfilling for us both. As I drove him to the hospital and then later helped my mother to care for him when he returned home, I felt a quiet peace at my center. I knew that I was giving him what he needed at that time, just as he had attended my needs when I was a child in his care. We may have exchanged roles in the "movie" my mother envisions, but there can be great satisfaction for all involved.

Likewise my brother acknowledges this role as he travels from Indiana to California at least twice a year, bringing with him his wife and two children whenever possible. He and I learned from our parents' example that as they and other loved ones reach that station in life, they don't want things: They want our time. Our honesty. Our love. I have learned that I am never more fully myself than when I forget my own nature in the joy and absorption of helping another family member.

Shortly after my father's recovery from surgery, my mother found among his papers a note he had written while in the hospital. Although the handwriting is shaky and the lines are crooked, the message is clear: "Yes, we're blessed with exceptional sons, ready to help without hesitation — with care and love toward the two of us. Thank God for giving them to us."

Selfless attention to the needs and happiness of an older family member is nowhere more beautifully illustrated than in the story of some friends of mine and their aging mother. Physically, she was small: about five feet two, perhaps. Upon first meeting her, I was impressed by her bearing — she was upright and her movements quick and agile. Her hands and feet matched her stature. She never fumbled, and her gestures were always expressive. Her bright eyes had a thoughtful, sober look, and their glance was penetrating, humorous, and warm.

She and her husband had been inseparable. Their mutual love for books and music became their life; they raised three children; and despite many setbacks, they endured as a loyal, loving couple. Her *joie de vivre* continually reminded me how much can be made of a lifetime.

But all that changed after her husband died, and she moved in with her daughter and son-in-law.

"You had him for fifty-one years," I said to her one day, not thinking.

"It wasn't long enough."

Over the next year Grandmama — as everyone affectionately called her — kept to herself in the back bedroom of the house, emerging only for meals, for solitary walks, or for occasional family gatherings at which she sat, by herself, in a distant corner. Crossword puzzles helped to pass the time, and many evenings her daughter would find her asleep in her chair next to the window overlooking the street, an unfinished puzzle dropped onto her lap.

Obviously she was grieving her loss, and no one was able to penetrate the wall fashioned of sadness and memories of a now distant past behind which she had retreated. Her grief had taken her to a place where her family could not follow. But still they gathered around, sat silently, and wept with her. They were fully present with her, but honored her silence, "a silence that," as poet Emily Dickinson said, "would be violated by too many words." I admired her daughter greatly for the way she opened her home to her mother, without any sign of impatience or complaint.

Then one day about a year later, a sudden change occurred in Grandmama's demeanor: a lightness to her step, a sparkle in her eyes, a slight, almost whimsical smile on her lips. One Sunday afternoon she revealed why. She had met a man, she said. He was seventy-six years old, himself recently widowed, and they had arranged to meet, for dinner, the following Friday.

"Wonderful!" I said when she told me the good news. "I'll drive you."

"Nope! It's all arranged. A cab will pick me up at 6:30, Friday."

On Monday afternoon her daughter took her out to buy a new dark blue dress (her favorite color) for the occasion. Thursday, she went to the beauty parlor to have her nails buffed and hair shampooed and set. Friday evening arrived. As all of us gathered on the front steps to watch as Grandmama climbed into the back seat of the yellow cab that would whisk her down the street and out of sight, I felt as my parents must have years before while watching me leave for the high school prom.

The next day my friend relayed Grandmama's account of that evening.

She had arrived at a West Los Angeles restaurant promptly at 7:30 P.M. The maître d' was expecting her, knew her by name, and said that her friend had not yet arrived. Would she like to take her seat — a special seat — in the back corner, away from the noise of the kitchen and the steady stream of customers? Grandmama said she would and sat down. And would she like a drink while she waited?

Now for as long as I knew her, Grandmama always had one drink a night, a scotch on the rocks. As my aunt used to say, there is something "very right" about a senior citizen drinking a scotch on the rocks.

So as she waited Grandmama had her drink. Now it was 8:00. She was not worried, but just a bit concerned. Still no sign of her friend. Perhaps he was caught in traffic?

The waiter approached. "Would you like to have your salad while you wait?"

Well, yes, she thought, she *was* hungry, and time was passing. Surely she could eat that and by then her date would arrive.

Now it was 8:25, and still no sign, not even a telephone

call, and understandably she was quite concerned. A seventy-six-year-old man out alone in a cab — perhaps there had been an accident? It had been drizzling when she left the house. Why hadn't he at least called? Well, she thought, no sense going hungry, and so for the next forty-five minutes Grandmama ate alone: dinner, dessert, then coffee. At 9:30, having grown ever more annoyed by her date's absence, Grandmama became convinced that she had been stood up. And all the way home she fumed. No call! Not even a message! A wasted evening! Wasted dress! Beauty parlor! And the more she thought of it, the angrier she became.

"All men are jerks!" she told my friend, outraged, at breakfast on Saturday. "I'll never speak to him again as long as I live!" And for the rest of the weekend that's all she talked of. You would never have known, to look at her, that this dynamo of righteous indignation was the same woman who only days earlier had been sunk in grief over a devastating loss.

When Monday morning arrived, there appeared to be a change in Grandmama, almost as if she had forgotten the incident entirely. Gone was the outrage, and in its place a now familiar lightness to her step, a certain twinkle in her eyes, a smile on her lips. When asked about her mood, she said nothing about the previous Friday, but only that she had a date, a dinner date, for next Friday evening.

"Wonderful!" I said, feeling somewhat like a character

out of Rod Serling's *Twilight Zone.* "I'll drive you!"

"No, no," she said, "all is arranged. A cab will pick me up Friday."

This time her daughter helped her pick out a red dress from her closet, a dress she hadn't worn in years. Thursday she went to the beauty salon to have her nails buffed and hair done. Friday, 6:30 P.M., the cab pulled up in front of the house, and Grandmama climbed in and was whisked away yet again for an adventure.

As I learned later, Grandmama arrived at the West Los Angeles restaurant right on time, 7:30. Yet again, the maître d' was expecting her, called her by name, and said that her guest had not yet arrived but would she like to take her seat — and on it went, almost an exact repeat of the previous week's scenario.

By 8:00, no appearance of the "mystery man," and once again, rising concern. Once again, salad, an entrée, dessert, coffee. Home in a cab by ten o'clock.

Once again, a weekend spent fuming. Once again, the pronouncement over breakfast Saturday: "All men are jerks! I'll never speak to him as long as I live!" And for the rest of the weekend the litany was repeated.

This went on for the next five years.

There *was* no mystery man.

There never *had* been.

Somehow, and for reasons we will probably never fully understand, in the deepest recesses of her mind and heart,

Grandmama had created — discovered? — an idealized friend. Why didn't we help her? The answer is obvious: We did. Her family and friends went along with it, as did the maître d', the cab driver, and the hairdresser. The cruelest thing anyone could have done would have been to say to her, even tenderly, "But Grandmama, there is no one."

What would have been the purpose? It might have shattered her. And to what end? All of us have illusions in which we need to believe. Who is to say that for Grandmama, this illusion was harmful? Rather, the contrary seems true. Grandmama lived as if the man were alive, and the Friday night melodrama allowed her to feel alive again, too. Those in her family respected her need for the guise and supported her with love and forbearance.

Sometimes candor isn't the best policy: Silence is. People of any age may have within their lives certain routines, certain secret anniversaries of the heart that help to sustain and encourage them, particularly in tough times. Like many elderly people, Grandmama had become childlike. She began to live in the past, which is safe, known, and lived through, unlike the future, which is unpredictable and therefore threatening. Better to construct a routine based upon the familiar than face the uncertainties of a life dramatically altered by change. By constructing and repeating her fantasy date, Grandmama had five rich years of something to look forward to each week, something to do, something to talk about.

And five years of delicious Friday dinners.

I am convinced that without the sustaining illusion of her always tardy gentleman — and without the support and tolerance of her daughter and family and friends — Grandmama would have had to endure the kind of lonely sadness Rainer Maria Rilke evokes in his austere poem, "The Poet":

> I have no one to love. I have no home.
> There is no center to sustain my life.
> All things to which I give myself grow rich
> and leave me spent, impoverished, alone.

Unfortunately, Rilke's lines describe all too many of the elderly in our society. Although some traditional cultures continue to emphasize the value of togetherness and solidarity, Western civilization increasingly embraces the values of independence and the autonomy of the individual. And the price is enormous: isolation and loneliness. In her wonderful book, *Another Country: Navigating the Emotional Terrain of Our Elders*, Mary Pipher writes, "Grandparents feel lonely and useless while a thousand miles away their grandchildren are not getting the love and attention they desperately need. There is a lot wrong with this picture."

A friend of mine recalls the time he visited a London convalescent hospital. He was amazed that all those poor aged people were so helpless, many of them abandoned and forgotten by the very children they had given life to and sustained. In bed after bed, he saw little white heads pressed against their pillows, some peeking just above the bedspread, many of them staring at him without expression, mouths open, others with eyes sad and haunted. One elderly couple — so gentle and wise and kindly — had been placed there when their children went on vacation, but after summer the children "forgot" to bring them back! Never before had my friend seen so many helpless people at one time for whom physical survival was such a daily challenge, loneliness such a daily misery.

As the doctor walked him past the many beds and explained the patients' illnesses, my friend prayed silently for each person. He later told me it was the most moving experience he ever had. He came away doubly aware of our responsibilities to our elders, and appreciating more deeply than ever that life is now, to be shared and to be grateful for. He thanked God for sending him there, and when he returned to his hotel, the first thing he did was call his parents back home in America.

"We must never forget that God has *allowed* them to live so long," he wrote to me a week later. "Old age is not a mistake. Or an accident. Or an oversight. It is the will of God. But it is not the will of God that so many of the aged are hidden away to languish under inadequate care with no friends or relations at all to visit them!"

Indeed, to honor age is to honor God. "You shall rise before the aged, and defer to the old," says Leviticus 19:32; "and you shall fear your God: I am the Lord."

Then I think of another friend: forty-one, an only child, married with three children of his own. His grandparents died when he was young, but his parents were very much alive, in their eighties, and for the past five years confined to a convalescent home about ten miles from where their son lives.

Each time I see him, I ask, "How are your parents?" And each time he responds, "Okay, I guess." What I have learned is that he rarely visits, hardly ever calls, and that neither his wife nor their children have anything to do with the aging couple at all — as if they are a secret shame, an embarrassment. When I ask him why, and when I pressure him — as a close friend can and should — about seeing his parents more often, he merely shrugs his shoulders and says something about the stress of work and home.

If I reflect upon this scene, I am reminded of F. E. Crowe, who called the aged of our time "perhaps the loneliest generation that ever inhabited the face of the earth." Or of Norman Cousins, who wrote, "The worst thing about being seventy-five years old is being treated as a seventy-five-year-old."

Unfortunately, abandonment is too often part of that treatment. Next to the fear of death, a universal fear and frequent reality of older people is being forgotten and alone when they are in a weak and vulnerable state. "Do not cast me off in the time of old age," pleads the Psalmist; "do not forsake me when my strength is spent" (71:9). Good food, efficient doctors, television, and quality care are all important. But for the elderly, nothing can substitute for the love of family and friends.

It seems that reverence for and consideration of the elderly have eroded for many reasons. Many families are splintered and dispersed, so that no one is nearby to attend to aging parents. Many communities have broken down, undermining the support of friends and neighbors. With significant exceptions, the media, the entertainment industry, and advertising all glorify the young while the elderly are frequently stereotyped, mocked, or exploited.

This prejudice against old age, which is underscored by the prodigious amounts Americans spend on products and services intended to make them look younger than they are, is ultimately self-destructive, for it denigrates the wisdom of our elders as simplistic or out-of-date and therefore forfeits the gifts they have to offer. Many young adults are the offspring of the so-called "Me Generation," which Christopher Lasch characterized as "the culture of narcissism." Perpetuating the busy, self-preoccupied, ego-centric world of their parents, they have no time for and little contact with their elders, no desire or sense of obligation to tend to their needs, and no clue about the gifts they could so easily receive through giving.

And baby boomers may be no better than their "Generation X" children, but for different reasons. As a generation, we haven't experienced nearly the hardships of our grandparents or parents. How extraordinary to think of living through the Depression (during which my maternal grandfather lost everything, including his first home) and of World War II, with all the attendant uncertainties. For many of us, the demand of caring for our aging parents is the first real test of our character. Beset by pressures from being sandwiched between their elders and their own children, some adult children may simply fail. It's easier to ignore their parents' needs or to pass their own responsibilities off to a senior center or nursing home.

What can we do about the problem? The answers are not clear-cut, and many caring, sensitive adults earnestly struggle with the very real dilemma of balancing the demands of their own lives with the increasing needs of their parents. Certainly we as parents can teach our children to respect elders, remembering that kids freely absorb our own attitudes. That means that we must first model that reverence ourselves. Further, we can ensure that our children know their grandparents and other relations as real human beings, not as indistinct entities with cameo appearances at Christmastime. We need to make the effort to include elders in our lives whatever their physical condition or living situation. Visits, phone calls, letters, even E-mail can make the child aware that his or her family is constituted of more than immediate parents and siblings. And we can expose young people to the aging population in other ways — in church and community activities, story time at school or the library, visits to hospitals or nursing homes. When children see elders as real people with interesting lives and fascinating stories to tell, they will be less inclined to believe the negative image of the aged portrayed in so much of the media.

One friend, whose father has suffered two strokes, wrote: "I've long ago admitted that there's not much I can do as I watch my parents ail and falter, but I still try to support them as well as I can. I struggle daily with the fine line between helping them when they really need it and inadvertently taking away large chunks of their independence. There's so much I'd like to 'fix' for them, but I also need to respect the fact that, like any adults, they want to keep as much control over their lives as they can. Unfortunately, there's no owner's manual that tells me how to do this; we're all traveling an unfamiliar road here."

As my friend has learned from the experience with her parents, we can immeasurably enrich their lives by visiting, calling, or writing. By listening and responding. By smiling at them. By sharing our own families and activities. By tending to small tasks that may seem so overwhelming to an older person. By sending a book or a magazine article or some snapshots. By being mindful of them and reaching out so that they know they are not alone. Such connections can yield a great harvest in return, for in connecting we are made aware of something we all too often lose sight of in our busy lives: We exist for each other.

My aunt used to say, "I'm not afraid of leaving this world. But I don't want to be stuck in some nursing home." That fear was shared by her parents (who indeed were able to remain at home until their last year of life) and now to some degree by my own. When my father expressed my mother's concern that if he goes first, she will be alone, my telephone call to her was swift and immediate: "That'll never happen," I assured her. "Let this be my burden."

I then sent her an anonymous prayer, which she taped to her refrigerator and reads every day:

> Let nothing ever grieve thee, distress thee,
> nor fret thee; heed God's good will, my
> soul be still, compose thee. Why brood all
> day in sorrow? Tomorrow will bring thee
> God's help, benign and grace sublime in
> mercy. Be true in all endeavor and ever ply
> bravely; what God decrees brings joy and
> peace. He'll stay thee. Amen.

We are our "brother's keeper," as the Scripture tells us, but in taking care of our fellow humans, we are caring for ourselves. For odds are that the crisis of old age is one we, too, will ultimately have to face. As Aristotle taught, pity for the plight of others requires our acknowledgment that the same ill could befall us. Surely it is not just kind but also wise to encourage respect for a condition we may well, in time, share.

The truth of this principle was impressed upon me in a particularly memorable way during the first eight years of my teaching profession, from 1973 to 1981, when I accepted along with my regular assignments two extra classes. My students were eager, attentive, actively involved — and all over seventy. They knew heart deep what only years of experience could give them. Remembering those seniors now, I think of the novelist James Michener's words: "The secret to a good life is to be around people who know something." Here were people who knew something.

After one particularly satisfying semester of instruction, my students gave me a print of Rembrandt's powerful painting *The Old Man Praying*. I have always loved that portrait, with its white-headed man in whose furrowed brow, sharp eyes, and brightly lit face I see such strength, such character, such wisdom. The print serves as a reminder of the vitality and depth of vision of those wonderful older students. Now, many years later, it also reminds me of those qualities in my parents and of their mortality, vulnerability, and fragility, and of the importance of honoring them while there is still time.

"Old age operates like the demise of a long relationship," wrote Rabbi David Wolpe, "even though we see it coming and watch its progress, its onset catches us by surprise." Yes, it has taken me a long time to accept the truth that my parents are slowing down. I don't know that I have fully accepted it, or that I ever will. One year, when they accompanied my own family on a trip, I couldn't help noticing that my father didn't seem to be having the same good time he had had on similar trips in the past. Since then I've become aware of other subtle signs, small changes that tell me his physical powers are diminishing. But I have to remember, as my mother keeps telling me, that they had very active lives for many, many years. Now they are interested in other things and don't feel the same need to move about.

But slowing down physically doesn't mean slowing down mentally. Our society's retirement policies are based on the absurd notion that human capacity falls off significantly at sixty-eight or seventy. It is unconscionable how often social pressures push people out of their jobs into increasingly early retirement. The loss of work has killed many. For men and women who have few interests outside of work, the first years after retirement are critical. Work helps to make people feel useful, needed, creative

— those most essential of feelings. In 1990, just a few days before his death by heart attack at seventy-seven, Norman Cousins wrote:

> No disease in the United States — not cancer, not heart disease, not diabetes, not multiple sclerosis — is more lethal than the boredom that follows retirement. The body goes into a state of rapid deterioration when it loses its reason for being, when mind and muscle are not put to use, and when the individual is surrounded by the perception of society that he or she no longer serves a useful purpose.

Right to the end, Cousins lived a full, active life. And, of course, so have countless others.

Fortunately, my parents developed good habits when young that continue to serve them in their old age. Their intellectual curiosity is still running strong, and reading continues to be a way of life for them. And my mother has her music. And her writing. For the past ten years, in project after project, I find reflected her utter *enthusiasm*, as one subject after another captures her interest, commands her study, and emerges from her imagination onto the typewritten pages. So it was in their youth, and so it has continued into their later years.

I call my parents at least twice a week, sometimes more often, and visit them with my wife and our son as often as possible. I am lucky: They live only one hundred miles away. I send them items in the mail. I think up projects for them. Seemingly small tokens can make a big difference in a life. And I pray for them daily — that God will continue to protect and provide for them, that He will care for them with tenderness and mercy. Left to themselves, my parents hold their lives in place by enjoying music, books, socializing, television, classes. But what they need in addition to these, what really infuses their days with warmth and meaning, is family.

In 1864 when the English poet Robert Browning wrote, "Grow old along with me! / The best is yet to be," he never dreamed that life expectancies in the West would rise over the next century from forty-four to seventy-six, with many surviving into their eighties and nineties. Far from being an embarrassment, old age is in fact a golden opportunity for human growth, fulfillment, and deep happiness. It opens the way for one to live more deliberately and serenely, apart from youth's passions and frivolities.

How privileged we are to be traveling through life with a select group composed of our parents and grandparents, aunts and uncles, cousins and other relations.

They widen our net in untold ways. They add depth and breadth to our experience as human beings. They shelter us, instruct us, guide us, enrich us. There is a reason — a divine reason, I believe — that certain individuals come into our lives. With a bit of effort and a lot of imagination, the task of caring for those that have become dependent and vulnerable can be seen not as a burden but as a joyful opportunity to connect and to love. Of course, helping may occasionally be inconvenient or difficult. Of course, there may be unpleasant or painful episodes. But we will never regret the choices we make to stay involved in their lives.

hearts undivided

What greater thing is there for two human souls,
than to feel that they are joined for life — to strengthen
each other in all labour, to rest on each other in all sorrow,
to minister to each other in all pain, to be one with each other in
silent unspeakable memories at the moment of lasting parting?

— GEORGE ELIOT

*A*mong the many obligations in life, the most important is the one we accept when we become husbands and wives. Marriage is more than a contract, a covenant, a convenience. It is sacrament, a serious life-long commitment, made "for better or worse" and — lest we forget — "in the presence of God."

Martin Luther once described marriage as a school for character. The large things are tested in the small things; or as Jesus said, those who are faithful in small things will be entrusted with large things. "In good marriages," wrote William C. Bennett, "men and women seek to improve themselves for the sake of their loved one. They offer and draw moral strength, day in and day out, by sharing compassion, courage, honesty, self-discipline, and a host of other virtues. Thus the whole of the union becomes stronger and more wonderful than the sum of the parts." Only in marriage, wrote Rabbi Harold S. Kushner, "can we meet our existential human need to transcend the loneliness of being an individual, to find the person who makes us whole, who provides us with what we lack and liberates the qualities hidden within us, and join with that person to 'become one flesh.'" For good reason, marriage is the first social relationship established in the Bible.

Other than life itself, one of the greatest gifts my own parents have given to my brother and me is the example of a stable, committed marriage. Letting us see that they loved and respected each other has been more important than anything they could have bought or done for us. With time, our confidence in their relationship set us free emotionally to get on with our own lives.

I had cause to reflect upon this in a most significant way in June 1999 when I visited them on the occasion of their fifty-fifth wedding anniversary.

Late that evening I was sitting in their living room

when my mother walked in and gently laid on my lap a packet of water-stained, light blue envelopes, tied up with pink satin ribbon.

"What's this?" I asked.

"Take a look!" she said.

I untied the ribbon, opened the first envelope, and withdrew the thinnest of white onionskin paper, folded in half. The date at the top of page one said June 3, 1943 — a year before they were married. I counted the letters: fifty-seven in all, still in their original postmarked envelopes.

"These are the letters I wrote to your father before and during the war. Well, not all of the letters, but many of them."

Now if given a choice between receiving a letter or a telephone call from a loved one, *always* my mother would choose the former — and so would I. A letter is tangible, usually written with care and over time, unlike telephone calls, which are impromptu and take less thought. Soon after receiving a telephone call we forget the words, the tone, the inflections; with a letter, it is all there for future generations to read and appreciate. With letters, we may honor memory. "Letters," said the poet John Donne, "mingle souls."

And so, letters as intimate as my mother's (along with a few of my father's) permitted me to slip away from present concerns, to open the door and step inside their earliest years together, before they married and established their family, before I was conceived.

Imagine! A packet of letters, treasured by my parents for more than five decades, now in my hands. My mother's gift was a vision of her I had seen but always from a different perspective, a vivid portrait of her even-handed, commonsense personality, of her frankness, her humor and wit — when she was only twenty years old! In reading them, I could virtually reconstruct (with her help) an engagement, a marriage, and a separation by war.

My father was commissioned in the U.S. Navy in May 1944. Two weeks later he and my mother were married and less than two weeks after that he reported to Wilmington, Delaware, for duty on the USS *LSM 211*. In November the ship loaded its cargo of five tanks and fifty-five officers and marines and sailed toward an undisclosed destination. During the next two years he wrote home every week.

Wartime mail delivery was sporadic, and both of my parents received each other's letters in bunches — two, three, sometimes four at a time, once thirteen in one day, and always two to three weeks after they had been sent. So neither knew what was happening with the other at just that moment, a disconnection alien to our current age of instant communication. For them, as for most families at the time, private correspondence became a kind of consolation, something to lean on as it was written, something to look forward to receiving, something to cherish and to read and reread. As poet Philip Larkin reminds us in "Aubade," "Postmen like doctors go from house to house," dispensing comfort, assurance, and healing.

My mother, who was living with her parents, would gather family members and even neighbors when she had composed a packet to send. They'd sit outside on the screened-in porch or, on cold wintry nights, the kitchen as a wood fire crackled in the stove, doors and windows shut tight against the cold. I can imagine my mother's cheerful voice as she read slowly and deliberately, her listeners savoring her accounts of everyday affairs: a movie, a new dress, church, shopping, plans for a wedding, visiting neighbors, cooking, taking walks, funny things seen or heard. In other words, my mother chose to emphasize not just her devotion and love for my father, but the stability, normalcy, and continuity of the home life he would one day return to.

Sometimes she quoted her own mother, as in, "When you are feeling low, do something for someone else, quick!" or "If you are down in spirits, name ten things for which you are grateful." Bible verses also appeared, most notably: "Cast all your care upon him; for he careth for you" and "I will not fail thee, nor forsake thee" (1 Pet. 5:7; Josh. 1:5, KJV).

In none of their letters is there any evidence of self-pity or complaint. Like my father, millions of servicemen and servicewomen had been separated from families and friends at the most sensitive stage in their lives, yet everyone was in the war together, united in an essential task against a common enemy. My father as well as my mother knew the enormous consequences resting on the war's outcome, and never for a moment doubted the nobility or rightness of the cause.

But in their letters nothing specifically was mentioned of the war: he couldn't, for security reasons, and she wouldn't ask. When the news came over the radio announcing that the invasion of Iwo Jima had begun, however, it was as if the radio had sent the family a personal message. Somehow they knew at that moment that he must be involved.

As my mother learned much later, approaching the island on February 19, 1944 — one day before my mother's birthday — his ship was hit in the hull by Japanese mortar fire. Somehow they reached shore, unloaded their tanks, cargo, and men, then left, all the while taking on water. Fortunately, the ship was built with some void compartments that enabled it to float with the stern of the ship four or five feet out of the water. A tug pulled the wounded, vulnerable vessel away at five miles per hour while the fighting raged on. Next morning they were towed to Saipan for repairs, then the ship limped to Honolulu and from there to California.

Although my father lost all of his belongings, including his college notebooks, clothing, and gear, when the ship flooded, somehow he salvaged the letters. When Japan surrendered in August 1945, the *LSM 211* was given orders to take special supplies to Wakayama, Japan, and finally returned to California in February 1946, at which time my father was released from active duty.

The letters survived for the very same reasons my parents' marriage survived over the years: My mother and father recognized something of value that should be treasured, preserved, and protected despite obstacles, or even tragedies. "Convenience" or "ease" never really entered into the equation. Like so many couples of that generation and since, my parents realized that when all frailties are revealed, a common bond can still hold the partnership together: commitment. Couples need to look beyond temporary irritation or frustration or even discomfort and focus on what brought them together in the first place — a sincere belief that life is, overall, better together than apart.

Over the years as I grew up, rarely did I hear between my parents any cutting words, though I'm sure they disagreed, even argued: All couples do. But never did I sense anything but the utmost respect for and devotion to each other. Individuals who were not fortunate enough to have had that model still can forge their own strong relationships if they act out of caring, kindness, and mutual regard.

The mystery is not that there is so much suffering in some marriages but why some collapse beneath it while others convert their pain into creativity and survival. We know that at least half of the marriages in America fail. We know or hear of couples who divorce after a single year — sometimes even less — of marriage, as well as couples who split after many decades. Might such relationships be redeemed rather than abandoned? The answer may lie within a relationship's specific history and the means the partners have discovered to deal with the difficulties inherent in the process of accruing that history together.

I found one example of how devotion can make a relationship endure in the lives of Neil and Jeanne Foster, whom I first met in 1963 when they were into their early forties. Ours became a close and confiding relationship, sustained by our correspondence and telephone calls along with visits each summer at their home in Colon, Michigan. On three occasions, Neil visited me in California.

They became like second parents to me, and for them I was like a son — a "foster son," as they liked to say. There was nobody else they felt close to. Other than one niece, whom Neil didn't get to know until later in adult life, and Jeanne's sister, Mildred, everybody they had loved in their lifetime was gone. And so in friends and neighbors they found the elements of a substitute family, along with (as I was to learn) countless other people drawn to and influenced by them.

On the surface they seemed happy and fulfilled, successful partners in a full life. But the surface is only that — surface.

In 1977, I spent Thanksgiving day with Neil and Jeanne. Neil was recovering from his first heart attack but was doing well, and after dinner we bundled up to go out for a walk. Jeanne, unable to bear the cold and too stiff to walk, stayed behind, peering through the frosted front room window.

Neil and I walked slowly, arm in arm, imagining the mist as the boundary between time and eternity. We walked into the mist, and came out the other side, and it was then that Neil told me the story of their "little angel."

Early in their marriage, Jeanne became pregnant. It was a time of great joy and expectation for both of them, and I cannot imagine a more loving set of parents. But it was not to be. In the second trimester severe complications developed and they found themselves faced with the excruciating decision between the life of the mother or the life of the child.

They prayed over this mightily, that there might be another choice, but there wasn't, and they had to act fast. So the child was aborted, a hysterectomy performed, and they grieved for the child that might have been and the children that never would be.

By mutual agreement, that child for which they silently longed was never mentioned again — although certain looks between them, certain messages over the radio or television, would cause them to sink into a reverie, and without asking each knew what had passed through the other's thoughts. Neil made me promise that I would not reveal to Jeanne what he had told me, and of course I agreed.

After our walk I planned to attend a gathering at an associate's house nearby, then drive back to Indiana the next morning where I was staying with friends.

"You're welcome to stay with us," Neil said. "After the party, drive by the house. If you see the porch light on, that means we're still up."

I went to the party fully intending to stay through the evening. But a soft inner tug beckoned me back, and within the hour I returned to Neil and Jeanne's house. The porch light was still on, so I climbed the front steps and rang the bell. Neil opened the door and I stepped inside.

"Welcome," he said, and embraced me. Neil's eyes met Jeanne's, and at that moment, as Neil confirmed later, they knew they were thinking the same thought: Their son had come home.

And so you can imagine, perhaps, my feelings two years later, on March 7, when I returned from work early in the afternoon, played back the message on my answering machine, and heard Neil's basso voice, firm but sad, come through with three sentences: "Hi, kid. We lost Jeanne this morning. I'll talk with you later."

From the sounds of voices in the background I understood that he had visitors. That night I had a long talk with Neil. He had faced many rough times, but this was the worst: "I know what it is to lose a mother and a dad; it's hard to lose your brothers, hard to lose your friends," he said. "But when you lose your mate, that's the toughest pill of all. That's very hard."

Yet partners like Neil and Jeanne can also find comfort in the very history they've created together. A month later, he and I were sitting on the patio behind his home, overlooking the "Enchanted Garden," as they called it. Because Jeanne's poor health had prevented them from traveling as much as they would have liked, they learned to love the garden and spent their summers working it. They had planted all of the trees and bushes when they moved to Colon in 1957. A statue of the Blessed Mary stood in their "quiet corner." Often they would say while sitting on the patio that no matter who went first, the survivor would always be able to find the other in the garden. That sense of constancy became a balm to him.

"She is still here," he said. "I feel her presence so strongly. I know she reminds me to take my pills at the right time. I hope this feeling will remain for quite a while as it is a great comfort. Oh, there are times I cry, but I do pray almost constantly." He began to tell me the story of her passing, but as he spoke, I saw in it the kind of tireless devotion and unshakable commitment that couples must work at if they want their marriage to be strong from the beginning and vital to the very end.

Neil told me of their early years, when they had toured with a school assembly show. How they loved that. Jeanne was the most active person, and they had such good times. But in 1958 Jeanne had a close brush with death when her lung collapsed as the result of a severe cold; they were forced to leave the road and for a year Neil worked in Chicago, then they moved to Colon. In their later years they developed a routine that provided independence but also, unfailingly, quiet, focused time together.

Their bond was so strong that they had worked out little signals between themselves. What may have appeared as casual interchanges to anyone else were, in reality, coded messages to each other. When, for example, Jeanne grew tired and wanted to return home from a dinner party, she had only to support her chin with her hand and look straight at Neil, her eyes narrowing. On other occasions a slight roll of her eyes conveyed to Neil her opinion of a guest's comment. Just a look or the tone of voice gave the other a clue.

"Don't ever be sad when I go," he told me. "I'm going to be the happiest person in that graveyard because I'll be with so many dear people," he said, referring to the family plot near Hinkley, Illinois, where Jeanne is buried next to his father and mother, with a space left for Neil. On the tree-covered hill also rest a brother, thirteen grandmothers, twelve grandfathers, and all of his uncles, cousins, and aunts, including the great aunt who helped to raise him.

hearts undivided

As he told me with almost unbearable poignancy, at six o'clock the night before she died, Neil helped Jeanne into the bathroom, where she stood, supporting herself by the sink. Neil turned to get one of her pills from the medicine cabinet and suddenly he heard an "ungodly sound, like a cannon going off." He spun around to find that she had fallen backward and was lying at his feet in her blue silk robe and pajamas. She gave Neil a terrified look, "like a wild animal that had suddenly hurt itself and couldn't understand why."

Neil dropped to his knees and said, "Oh honey, what has happened?" He held her head and shoulders in his arms and tried to calm her down. Eventually they determined she wasn't injured and Neil was able to help her up and out into the living room, where they resumed their usual evening routine, though somewhat shaken. They ate, watched TV, and went to bed.

For many years they had slept in separate bedrooms because of Jeanne's health problems. So the next morning Neil went in to rouse her and noticed that she was lying slumped over on her side, partly uncovered. He spoke to her, and she said four words to Neil, very faintly.

After that Jeanne failed fast. She was restless and incoherent, and by the time the doctor arrived, barely conscious. She died within the hour.

So Neil was alone. He sat on the edge of the bed, put his cheek next to hers, hugged her close, and prayed. He told her that he loved her so much. "You've gone to heaven now," he whispered. "It won't be long and I'll be with you, I promise you." He held her for quite a long time, crying.

"She was so cold," he said, "but I knew she wasn't in pain anymore. I knew her spirit, her soul wasn't there any longer. I knew this was just the shell that was left."

Soon the funeral home staff came and took Jeanne's body away. "The house was so empty," Neil said. "I felt so alone." But through the memorial service and burial, Neil felt the support of friends.

"I didn't cry," he said. "But I prayed hard, and found out later that a lot of people were praying for me, too, and that's what carried me through." At the cemetery, he later remembered, "I didn't feel like I was leaving her alone," he told me. "I felt like I had taken her home."

"Nothing gold can stay," wrote Robert Frost in a poem by the same name, a reality we must face in relationships as we do in life. To experience the joy of love is to invite the agony that will inevitably come when the loved one is taken away. To fasten our affection on anything or anyone is to lay our head on the block. Yet we must do so, or be condemned to a life without companionship, compassion, or comfort.

When we choose the union of our soul with another's, we are inviting in all of life's eventualities — its losses as well as its gains, its sorrows as well as its joys. Those who abandon this commitment when difficulties arise also leave behind the growth and enrichment that can come from weathering stormy seas. "Seldom, or perhaps never," wrote Carl Jung, "does a marriage develop into an individual relationship smoothly and without crises; there is no coming to consciousness without pain."

Most of us when we marry face enormous interpersonal struggles. Different cultures, different outlooks on the world, different challenges, different expectations — all of these can cause a rift between members of a couple that can seem at times unbridgeable. But bridge that gap we must. How? How can two people learn to perform as a single unit, continue to love one another and become — as the Bible says — "one flesh"? This is perhaps "the most difficult task of all, the epitome, the ultimate test," said the poet Rainer Maria Rilke. "It is that striving for which all other striving is merely preparation." We marry strangers; and it takes years before we see the whole person. I am sure that many couples would agree with Anne Morrow Lindbergh when she wrote in *Dearly Beloved* nearly thirty years after her wedding day: "Only two real people can meet. It took years of stripping away the illusions, the poses, the pretenses,...[and] this was why...you could never regret the past, call it a waste, or wipe it out."

What can help to hold couples together, I believe, is a shared faith in God, and a clear-eyed view of their own and their partner's limitations. That means accepting without bitterness the flaws and imperfections of the other, and praying that our partner accepts our own flaws as well. That also means thanking God for our mate's — as well as our own — strengths, knowing that in each other we will find resilience where we separately are weak. On the other hand, we must not depend on our spouse to carry our entire emotional load, for unrealistic expectations foster unmet needs and unresolvable conflicts. Marriage is truly a partnership, and the couple must work together for the benefit of the new entity — the family — they joined forces to establish.

When the storms come, it may be tempting to become bitter, to strike out against each other or even against God. But a couple must avoid the temptation to succumb to pain or frustration and lash out. Instead, adversity should help the partners draw together, not pull apart. Neil and Jeanne grew closer to one another with each difficulty and evermore trusting in God to pull them through.

Prayers, reading, studying, speaking, and writing can serve ultimately to help couples to know God better, and as a result there is less basis for anxiety or fear, less reason for pretense or lies. God can become a still point where our life together is mutually anchored and from which we can as one reach out to others with hope and courage and confidence.

Most evenings Jeanne could be found sitting up in bed reading from the *Book of Common Prayer.* "This, too, will pass away" became one of the couple's favorite consolations, as did John's words from his Gospel: "What no eye has seen, nor ear heard, nor the heart of man conceived,...God has prepared for those who love him" (1 Cor. 2:9, RSV). Their faith in God and in the strength of their marriage extended beyond the vicissitudes of life and even, at the last, beyond death.

I wondered for a long time what four words Jeanne spoke to Neil before she slipped from him, what phrase or sentence or knowledge she wanted to impart as her final gift to the faithful partner in her lifelong journey. For awhile I couldn't really guess what she said, but now, after thinking about the lessons their lives taught me and the model their marriage set forth, I think I know. Jeanne had said, "I see our child."

More than ever, our torn world needs these kinds of marriage as examples of what relationships can be. The long, happy marriages I have described are not just for the two partners experiencing them. They are for all of us. As we consider the love and the sharing and the encouragement these individuals gave to each other, we might come to understand that this sometimes sorry world has not yet fallen apart. Rather, the Love that started life at the very beginning has the power to hold it together until the very end.

The transformative power of marriage is recorded, I believe, in my parents' wedding photograph, a copy of which hangs in our family room at home. Although my Aunt Myrtle could not leave her military post to attend the service, a week after receiving a print she sent a congratulatory letter to her younger sister (my mother): "The picture shows me an expression that I've been waiting to see," she wrote. "It's hard to put a name to it — maturity sounds too hard boiled, though I think really that's what it is. I cannot help feeling that it's the outcome of your feeling for Stan — a latent dignity and sense of well-being that shows on your face."

On occasion a friend will ask me why I waited until I was thirty-four to get married (as if I had any say in the matter). The answer is easy: I hadn't met Patti until I was thirty-one!

When my wife and I look back upon our own eighteen years of marriage — short by comparison to the examples in this chapter — it seems to have passed in one long flash. Of course, time does play tricks on us and the business of day-to-day living is far more complicated than that. As our pastor predicted, there have been illnesses, sometimes impatience, and disappointments, but as we have seen in the time we have been together, the God who called us together has given us the power, the grace, and the healing to accomplish the vows that we took on March 19, 1983.

In Harper Lee's *To Kill a Mockingbird,* Atticus Finch offers his daughter the following advice: "If you can learn a simple trick, you'll get along a lot better with all kinds of folks. You never really understand a person until you consider things from his point of view...until you climb into his skin and walk around in it."

It is clear that many successful couples have discovered that secret early in their own marriage. We all have unique visions of the world. No two people look at the physical world in exactly the same way. None of us, says Father Thomas Keating, has "immaculate perception." Every eye sees differently. Many problems within marriages are caused when couples forget this simple but profound truth.

There are no doubt as many answers to the question about what makes marriage succeed as there are couples, but from Scripture as well as the examples I have cited, I believe we can find some absolutes. Couples must share a lifelong commitment to each other, to their marriage, and to their home. (I remember a friend telling me, "You don't *marry* the right person. You *become* the right person!") In addition, they must constantly work to contribute faithfulness, unreserved love, sexual fulfillment, tender respect, and mutual submission. *To submit* in

Greek means to voluntarily offer oneself as a student servant: In a very real sense, partners must willingly and freely serve each other. Marriage is also a spiritual companionship in which both partners acknowledge their dependence upon God. Indeed, the key to compatibility, said my pastor, is to invite God into the mix and say, "Change us to love each other.... See your mate as God's gift and the one you are supposed to practice the love of God on."

For marriage has been instituted by God for the well-being of all humankind. Through His disciples and through the Scriptures, He has instructed those who enter this relationship how they are to love and care for one another. In his letter to the church at Ephesus, Paul described the relationship of the Lord to the church as a symbol of what marriage ought to be. We remember His sacrifice, His love for us, His caring for us, His restraint from judging us, and His steadfastness in upholding and encouraging us. So must the relationship of one to the other be in a marriage: blessed by Him to be united in a mystical way physically, spiritually, emotionally, heart deep. Two become one, through the blessing and grace of God Himself.

As the pastor charged my wife and me during our wedding ceremony, "As you love one another, remember, it's not just for you. It's part of God's plan. It's for the sake of God's people and a very torn world that needs your kind of love."

a child's innocence

Backward, turn backward, O Time, in your flight;
Make me a child again, just for tonight.

— Elizabeth Chase Akers

You think your marriage is good now?" a colleague said to me one day. "Wait until you have your child!"

How right she was. If we so choose and are indeed blessed to have or adopt children, there is nothing quite like the sheer enjoyment we feel as we delight in them, rejoice with them, have good times together, and treasure the privilege of nurturing and guiding them.

For my wife, Patti, and me, the adventure began on the evening of August 5, 1988. We had prepared well for the birth by attending the Lamaze classes and practicing the exercises together, reading every recommended book we could find, and watching as Patti blossomed with the child she was carrying.

But it was truly a magical moment when, after seven hours of labor, a new reality set in and I saw the crown of our son's head emerge and then his tiny body slide easily and cleanly into my waiting hands. At that instant an unexpected wave of love flowed through me so powerful it was nearly overwhelming. And as I cut the umbilical cord and then lifted our son and placed him gently onto Patti's stomach, I knew that we had experienced something deep. How important it is in the years ahead, when frustrations and challenges are certain to rise, that we remember this time of first profound love.

Three days later when Patti and Ryan were allowed to leave the hospital, I found myself thinking, "You mean we get to keep him?" I felt as if I was bringing home a precious piece of crystal — reminding me of the times I had driven with my ninety-one-year-old grandmother riding in the backseat. Every bump in the road made me nervous!

And when my mother commented later that evening over the telephone, "Now you have your family safe at home," I felt a tie both to that tiny, defenseless newborn sleeping in my arms and to her years of experience. From that moment I began to better understand how essential my parents were to my own (and my brother's) well-being and innocence. Not until we become parents ourselves do we realize how much our parents loved us and sacrificed for us.

Since the day Ryan became part of our family, the experience of raising a child has opened up in me a dimension that I didn't know I had — that of the nurturing, protective father. It came unexpectedly and sweetly settled upon me like the gentle touch of a dove; suddenly I was confronting and questioning society's long-held assumptions about detached fathers and discovering more deeply than I had imagined possible what it is to love another and to bond so profoundly.

One of the ways we can fulfill the calling to care for such precious gifts is to spend time in play with our children and include them in our social and professional lives. Children need to know that they are an essential part of the family unit, not just peripheral or secondary to their mother and father's relationship. While a husband and wife's quality time together, alone, is essential to a healthy marriage, it is also important that children develop early on a sense of togetherness. Their needs, wants, interests, hopes, and expectations should be components of the overall family dynamic, for all members' lives are inescapably intertwined from birth to death. As parents we should not only enjoy, experience, and be grateful for life in every moment, but we should teach that attitude of reverence and gratitude to our children by showing it to and sharing it with them. With a few important exceptions, what task worth doing cannot include in some way our own children?

Every year just after Christmas it has been my wife's custom to join me at a four-day literary conference, each time in a different city. For the first three years after Ryan was born, we left him with Martie, his maternal grandmother. Each year that became a little harder for us to do. We found ourselves saying, "Ryan would love to see this!" or "I wonder what Ryan is doing right now?"

When he turned four, Ryan wanted very much to go with us to New York City, but once again we decided to leave him behind. His grandmother put together an ingenious way for him to measure the time. Into a vase she placed five long-stemmed red roses. Each morning he removed one. When the vase was empty, he knew we were returning.

While that ritual may have made our time away easier for Ryan, it wasn't any easier for us, and on our way home I said to Patti, "This is the last time we take such a trip without him."

Since then we have shared our joy of travel with him on many occasions, and I can only begin to imagine how he has been affected by what he has seen and heard. Most of all, I believe, subtle messages of belonging and being "counted in" have registered in his soul.

We have all heard of the empty nest syndrome suffered particularly by mothers when their children leave home for college or marriage. Many fathers suffer, too, from profound regret over missed opportunities to be with their children *as children,* and from their shocked realization of how little they really know them. That is an irretrievable loss, a tragedy for both child and parent.

"Where did all the years go?" a friend asked me one day after seeing his son off to college. "Too often I had left home before he was up, and returned after he was asleep. All those missed recitals and ball games and bedtime stories. Those years I can never replace. If I had to do it over again, I would have spent more time with my children."

Sometimes, of course, the demands of work require husbands or wives to be separated from their children for long periods. But with 168 hours in a week, surely there is available to us more than the national average of seven minutes per week of quality time between parents and children!

As parents we must be always attentive to the potential for that time together and its significance in our children's and in our own lives. Rearranging a meeting, rescheduling a travel date, staying at the office a bit late or leaving a little early, rising early on a weekend, setting the newspaper aside, or putting the TV remote down: These are not big sacrifices to make for the well-being of our children and the quality of our relationships with them. By giving a little we gain much, for, if we take the time to look, we may just be lucky enough to see the world through a child's eyes again, and that is a rare good gift indeed.

A child is blessed with an inherent innocence and a vast capacity for wonder, and parents are called to preserve that innocence for as long as possible. It is better for the children, better for the family, better for the world. Soon enough children will have to deal with life's exigencies, but the period during which they can live safely within the immense realm of unlimited possibility develops in them an inner strength and a capacity for joy that can serve them throughout life. How thoughtless, or at worst how cruel, it is for an adult to undermine those gifts. That truth has been impressed upon me many times.

Once, when Ryan was eight years old, he joined me on a weeklong business trip to Little Rock, Arkansas. No sooner had we checked in, retreated to our hotel room, and begun to unpack, than he exclaimed,

"Daddy, my tooth came out!"

Sure enough, a bottom left molar that had been growing ever looser over the previous week now lay in his outstretched open hand. What number was that? I'd lost count, but as we have always done, we made plans to put it under his pillow for the tooth fairy's visit. And because this was the first time that Ryan had lost a tooth so far away from home, he wanted to write an extra special message:

"Are you the same tooth fairy that comes to our home?" he wrote on a sheet of the hotel's stationery. Then he left a space to check off either "Yes" or "No." At the bottom he added: "P.S. Please sign your name."

Then he slipped the note into a Ziploc bag along with the tooth, and soon we went to bed.

Upon waking the next morning, Ryan retrieved the bag from under his pillow and pulled out the note. There, in bold red ink, was a check mark next to "Yes," and in a rather hurried cursive handwriting, the signature, "Tooth Fairy." Slipped into the bag along with the note was a crisp ten dollar bill. The tooth was gone.

"Wow!" I said, recalling the delight I had felt as a child under similar circumstances. "The best I ever got was twenty-five cents. Ten dollars! That's more than you ever get at home!"

I have never seen Ryan more gleeful than when he shared this event with his mother over the telephone or, later that morning, with the committee members at my meeting. All of them responded with elaborate admiration, except for one individual, who, shaking his head and frowning, said,

"Well, it's a pleasant enough fantasy for a child. I believed in the Tooth Fairy too, until one day when I found all of my teeth in a box in my mother's closet!"

An audible groan went through the room as he said this, but fortunately I had sensed where he was headed by the time he got to the word "fantasy," and distracted Ryan momentarily by leaning over and whispering in his ear, "They really like your story!"

"What did he say?" my son asked.

"Oh, he was talking about his childhood," I said, and then quickly changed the subject.

Why did that man feel compelled to say that?

That story could symbolize many instances when adults shatter some childhood fantasy and as a result rob a child of some of his or her innocence.

The Russian poet Korney Chukovsky describes a policy instituted in the 1960s by the Soviet government eliminating all fantasy from the education of children in favor of simple, realistic, factual stories. Then one of the major Russian educators began to keep a diary of her own child's development. She found that her child, as if to compensate for what he was being denied, began to make up his own fantasies. He had never heard a fairy tale, never heard a folktale, but his imaginative world was peopled with talking tigers, birds, bugs, beautiful maidens, castles, and underground cities. Chukovsky concluded, "Fantasy is the most valuable attribute of the human mind and should be diligently nurtured from earliest childhood."

Think, for example, of all a child learns about the world from a belief in Santa Claus and all that we learn about the soul from those who share that belief: of our need for love and laughter, family and togetherness, belonging and sharing, paying attention to little things. "Blessed be the hand that prepares a pleasure for a child," says Douglas Jerrold, "for there is no saying when or where it may bloom forth."

How clearly I remember the efforts my parents expended to perpetuate the myth of Jolly Old Saint Nicholas! How wonderful that they cared so much to create, sustain, and respect this fantasy for me. As a parent myself I now understand how much delight they derived from seeing my excitement as we prepared for the holiday, my anticipation on Christmas Eve, and my wide-eyed joy that morning. Something very special rises in the soul of a child when he realizes much later that his parents have conspired to play this elaborate game for his benefit.

Such children have much more than magical moments to cherish; they also have a deeply ingrained sense of worth, a lasting affirmation of how important their welfare and happiness are to the family as a whole and their parents in particular. And they learn what joy comes from giving joy.

Like many families, my wife and I have developed various preparations to make Christmas and Santa's expected visit special for our child. A week beforehand, Ryan calls "Santa Claus" on the telephone to place his wish list. It's always a memorable time, and I must admit my mind and heart leap back to my own childhood when I overhear the deep, loving tones on the other end and see in Ryan's eyes and hear in his voice such sweetness and faith. On one occasion he heard a yell in the background at the other end of the line.

"Daddy, I heard one of the elves!" Ryan exclaimed after hanging up. "He was calling for Santa while we were talking!"

On Christmas Eve, Ryan and his mother bake two dozen chocolate chip cookies: twenty for us, four for Santa. These, along with an ice cold glass of milk, some carrots (for Rudolph), and a handwritten note, are set up on a table close to the open fireplace. Then we go to bed, knowing — as our son reminds us — that if we catch Santa in the act of delivering presents, he will disappear without leaving anything.

One year, just before midnight and long after Ryan had gone to bed, I crept upstairs to his room to check on him as I do every evening before retiring. He was lying on his side, covers up to his chest, asleep, or so I thought. I walked in softly, bent down, gently kissed his cheek, and said, "Good night, Ryan. I love you."

Suddenly he sat straight up, breathing heavily, wide eyed.

"Oh Daddy, it's you!" he said with undisguised relief. "When I heard footsteps and felt my blanket move, I thought it was Santa Claus making sure I was asleep. I was too scared to even breathe!"

Why have these and other traditions like birthday celebrations or Halloween lasted for so long in so many cultures? Because they feed a hunger to believe and fantasize and create that is in every child. These traditions, fantasy figures, and stories have been "honed and polished and perfected," writes psychologist Bruno Bettelheim, "by the minds and spirits and needs and wisdom of millions of people across hundreds, perhaps thousands, of years." As parents I believe we are called to honor them, and thereby honor the child.

Many of the themes of these practices and stories are imbedded in classics of literature that reinforce childhood innocence. Heroes and villains are easily identified. Good actions are rewarded and bad ones punished. Right prevails, wrong fails. The people worthy of emulation are kind, steadfast, selfless. The stories of the Brothers Grimm or Hans Christian Andersen, of Charles Perrault or Lewis Carroll, to name a few, appeal to the very best instincts in a child and reflect the very noblest in our culture. They contribute to the child's mind — called by Plato "a land of health, amid fair sights and sounds," which, he continued, should "receive the good in everything; and beauty, the effluence of fair works, shall flow into the eye and ear, like a health-giving breeze from a purer region."

Besides depicting an ideal moral universe, these stories are also a magic mirror that reflects some aspects of the child's innermost self. Immerse a child in these tales and the visions they communicate, and the youth's inner world becomes what Bettelheim calls "a deep, quiet pool" in which he or she soon discovers ways to gain peace both within and without. Our obligation as adults is to listen to their messages, to retell them, and thereby to pass them on to our children, says Bettelheim, "so that there will not pass from our future the enchantment that begins with the honored words, 'Once upon a time, long ago and far away, in a deep forest, there lived a child — much like you.'"

"Especially with children," writes John M. Drescher, "small things wear the garments of greatness."

Certainly a major enemy of a child's innocence and sense of wonder — and no friend to a family's connectedness — is the stupefying incursion of television into the privacy of our homes, our gathering places, even our schools. If so many people didn't depend upon the entertainment industry for a living, I would love to turn off all televisions for a year — and then see what happens. The medium should occupy a minor role in our lives; for many, however, it is a major player that leaves no time for anything or anyone else. Life is short, relationships priceless. Time spent in front of the screen is lost forever.

Recently I heard a radio advertisement for a Father's Day gift. For only $199, the ad said, children could buy Dad a satellite dish that will give him 145 additional channels to watch.

"Yes," I said to myself, "and 145 more reasons to tune out his children!"

I am thankful that I have never had a reason to become addicted to television, and I credit my family in large part. For one thing, my parents didn't acquire a set until I was ten years old, and then they carefully monitored and limited my viewing. The TV never became the center of our family's interactions or my play hours. By the time a television came into our home, I so enjoyed reveling in my own imagination, in my own way of working and playing and thinking, that the tube seemed to me merely a distraction to be avoided most of the time.

But that attitude is harder to find in our electronic, wired — and now wireless — age. Today in the average home the set is on six hours per day. Over two million children under the age of eleven are still watching it at midnight. A typical first grader has seen 5,000 hours of TV programming — which is enough cumulative time to earn a college degree. And how disheartening it is that by the time the average student reaches high school, he or she has witnessed 100,000 televised acts of violence. "Parents can no longer control the atmosphere of the home," wrote Allan Bloom, "and have even lost the will to do so." What "innocence" can endure in the face of such an onslaught?

Innocence, indeed. Enchantment is sacrificed on the altar of "entertainment," youthful ideals and sensitivities undermined by the gore of "reality-based programming." We have all read stories of the desensitization of young children to violence. That reality was brought home recently to a friend of mine. Her twelve-year-old daughter was sunbathing by the pool outside of their apartment building one day when suddenly she heard a terrible screech of tires, a dull but loud thud, and a release of air.

She got up from her lounge, looked over the wall, and saw at the intersection the remains of two badly mangled cars that had collided head-on. Without another thought she returned to her chair and lay down. Ten seconds later she realized what she had done, bolted from the lounge, and ran to the telephone to call 911.

"Imagine," my friend said to me later. "At first, my daughter didn't even comprehend the enormity of what she had seen. It was almost as if she had been watching a television show or a movie. Her mind interpreted the scene as 'unreal' or 'staged.' She said she even wondered why she wasn't hearing music!"

A colleague of mine related how her five-year-old granddaughter uses the word *hate* whenever registering dislike of anyone or anything: "Oh, I hate family meals!" or "I hate that movie!" or "I hate to do that!"

"One wonders," I commented, "where she heard the word *hate.*"

To which my colleague responded (with no sense of irony), "Oh, one can't live in this society without hearing it. It's used all the time on TV." Consider how thoroughly the phrase "I hate it when that happens" has permeated our culture; it originated as a punchline in an old *Saturday Night Live* sketch.

For good reason, anthropologist Margaret Mead once referred to television as the "Second Parent." Many children currently spend more time with television than with their fathers.

Now a new electronic incursion threatens the impressions of children, isolates family members literally for hours, and invites graphic words and images on virtually any subject into our homes. The explosion of Internet usage is an unprecedented event whose ramifications are still far from clear. What is clear, however, is that relatively young children with basic computer skills can avail themselves of a frightening array of Web sites on such topics as pornography, hate groups, weaponry, and drugs. Cases have already been documented in which children have been victimized by predators through chat rooms and other E-links.

Of course, there are also many excellent sites for children, full of information intended and shaped for young minds. And the value and potential of the Net as a vehicle for the exchange of information and opinion is indisputable. But to allow a child free, unlimited, and unmonitored access to the Internet is to open wide the door of our home to any and all strangers who might wander in from the street. Some might have wonderful, uplifting tales to tell; others might teach lessons a child should never learn.

To these ubiquitous distractions we could add, of course, many other parts of our culture that, if uncontrolled, can suppress the imagination and erode the protective dividing line between the innocent child and the experienced adult. Consumerism, and its consequent loss of delayed gratification, is one — as children are taught that satisfaction can be derived from buying almost anything.

Lack of parental attention is another. Some trends in our educational system (unconscionably overcrowded classrooms, declining authority, uncertified teachers, lowered academic standards, absence of prayer) are others.

Our nation's obsession with spectator sports is another tide washing away the fragile shores of unspoiled childhood simplicity. Like most youngsters, in school both my brother and I were active athletes. I qualified for the varsity wrestling team in high school, and participated in intramural basketball, volleyball, track, and swimming. Thanks to my father's vision and influence, everyone in our family learned to play golf, and some of my happiest memories are the many hours spent together on the course. We also went together to all of the Purdue University football and basketball games, and now each fall my son and I return to Indiana to be with his cousins while Glenn and I attend homecoming.

But never did sports so dominate our lives that everything and everyone else of importance was ignored. Kids in peewee leagues are reduced to tears when they discover not everyone can be a "star" like the players on TV. A few dollars an hour in an entry-level position becomes unacceptable to a young person who reads about multimillion-dollar signing bonuses or product promotion deals. Logo merchandise — none of it cheap — becomes the required uniform at school. All of these phenomena underscore the negative effects the crass commercialism of professional sports can render on our youth. Instead of heroes in sports they see marketable media commodities. Such emphasis on the bottom line can obscure the very real benefits that participating in and watching sports can produce.

Most children want to live as deeply as they can; they want to know themselves, their siblings, and their parents, and other relations and friends. It is our obligation as parents to create and sustain an environment that helps them to do just that. But that requires time to play, loving attention, encouragement, imagination, and effort. We must limit our children's exposure to the media, and monitor carefully what they are exposed to. Otherwise, the distractions of electronic entertainment and the consumer mentality will take them away from others and themselves and their family, impose on their psyches scattered images that seldom have any direct relation to who or what they are as individuals, and leave them with no time or incentive to look within or to reach out.

If you doubt this, then consider two questions: When was the last time that, after hours of watching car chases, surfing the Internet, or playing Nintendo, your child came away with greater self-knowledge? And when was the last time that he or she came away from these electronic distractions a *happier* person — not amused, not entertained, but happier?

A child's mind is, if we allow and encourage it to be, a wellspring of hope, joy, curiosity, exuberance, magic, faith, and unfettered potential. On this Plato had much to say in his *Republic:*

You know that the beginning is the most important part of any work, especially in the case of a young and tender thing; for that is the time at which the character is being formed and the desired impression is more readily taken....Shall we just carelessly allow children to hear any casual tales which may be devised by casual persons, and to receive into their minds ideas for the most part the very opposite of those which we should wish them to have when they are grown up?

We would never inject our children with some substance that might render their senses numb to the tart crispness of a freshly picked apple, the cool relief of a clear lake's waters on a hot August day, the solid comfort of a parent's arm resting protectively on a shoulder. Neither should we deaden their imaginations or anesthetize their capacity for wonder. Children need childhood.

One way we can encourage our children's remarkable capacity for wonder is to lead them in the direction of a hobby, some activity that is uniquely theirs to study, own, practice, enjoy, and share. Like many young boys and girls, I developed an early love for the art of magic. When

I was five years old, my family moved to Chadbourne, a student residence hall on the University of Massachusetts campus, where my father was a faculty resident. Apart from my school pals, most of my friends were college students. I played baseball with them in the quadrangle, did my homework with them in one of their rooms, and set up carnivals and game shows in their recreation room.

One of the students, Mr. White, was also a magician, and one day (after my repeated pleas) he showed me two tricks: how to "vanish" a half-dollar and how to "change" a scarf from green to yellow just by pulling it through my fist. The thrill of discovery I experienced that afternoon has stayed with me all of my life, and there's never a time as a performer or as a spectator when I don't reexperience it.

My father had a copy of G. S. Ripley's *Magic for Boys* (a title which, in our enlightened era, would have to be altered!). Each evening my mother and I learned how to put together the materials for one of the tricks and then how to perform it. At age ten I debuted my act and was paid two dollars plus a twenty-five cent tip. My parents had hired me for my own birthday party!

A classified advertisement in the local newspaper — "Magician for All Occasions. Call Dale Salwak" along with my telephone number — brought me additional work, and slowly my reputation, and confidence, grew. Apart from the obvious financial gains, performing magic helped me overcome my shyness and my fear of speaking in public. It became a way of exploring and developing my creativity. And it gave me a reason to want to stay home, with something new to learn, while some children seemed always to be looking for things to do.

Magic has many other applications in the life of a child. I have had the privilege of working with Aubrey Fine, Ed.D., a licensed psychologist and director of special populations at California Polytechnic University, who has developed a program (The Magic Within You) designed to help children who suffer from learning disabilities or hyperactivity and who are at risk of developing low self-esteem.

After twenty weeks of instruction in the basics of the art, imagine what it is like for a previously angry, defiant child to come smiling into the classroom dressed as a magician. Under his arm he carries a "magic box" loaded with the tricks that he has made. He now believes that his mind, like a magic wand, can make the impossible possible.

In front of parents, fellow students, and staff, he performs a ten-minute show, featuring the five tricks with which he feels most confident. In doing so, he has learned to take control of himself. He has developed a positive self-image. He has been taught a process that he will use over and over again throughout life. In discovering how to perform a magic trick for others, he is also discovering that he has the magic within him — to do anything that he wants to do.

Magic, too, is a wonderful leveler. Over the years I

have met people from all professions, all educational and economic backgrounds, and instantly, when we discover our mutual love for the art, potential barriers or defenses drop — and we become lifelong friends.

Now I see a similar interest growing in my son, Ryan. When he turned four, on occasion he would slip into my rehearsal studio, sit in his director's chair, and watch quietly (sometimes while dressed in his pj's and oversized koala bear slippers). Soon he began to work his way to my props tray and try to duplicate what he saw with a coin or deck of cards.

At five, he began to accompany me to some of my performances, always sitting in the wings, again in his director's chair, watching my show. When he turned seven, I built for him a duplicate set of my own props, all sized to his hands. As I slipped on my tuxedo, he put on his and then led me downstairs to the stage entrance. He watched every show from the wings, often trying to emulate with his own props what he saw me do, and then helped me clear the stage once the curtain had closed. Now he is a vital part of my performance.

"Daddy, how many shows do we have tonight?" he asked one evening.

"Two," I said.

"Oh, I wish we had a hundred!"

Parents can share an almost limitless range of activities with their kids — hobbies and skills that can provide lifelong opportunities and interest. It's an easy matter to show your son or daughter how to cast a fishing lure (you might duck on the first few tries!) or how to swing a tennis racquet. A child's interest might be piqued by stamps, baseball cards, or other collectibles. Why not include the child in fixing your car or planting flowers? Camping or hiking could open a whole world of enjoyment. A set of watercolor paints and some paper are very small investments to make in a child's creativity, stimulation, and sense of worth.

My wife and I love the theater, and we've made a point of taking Ryan to musicals and dramatic productions suitable for his age: *Joseph and the Amazing Technicolor Dreamcoat, Beauty and the Beast, The Wizard of Oz, A Christmas Carol.* As he's grown, we've expanded the scope of the productions we've exposed him to. Every community has local theaters and drama groups performing a rich array of theatrical genres. Think of how our children's understanding of the power of language to entertain and enlighten is enhanced as they sit, transfixed, watching *The Importance of Being Earnest* or *The Glass Menagerie.* And they will soak it in, if we simply expose them to it.

Afterward, try to visit the cast backstage, and once in the greenroom take a step backward and let your children walk alone into the middle of the actors, be greeted, and have a chance to talk with them. Exposure to both sides of theatrical life — from the audience and from the stage — allows the child to see the faces behind the "masks," the reality behind the pageant, something no television show on Earth can do.

In other words, what we are doing with Ryan is what our own parents did for us and what I would encourage all parents to do with their own children — and that is, expose them to the best that our culture has to offer, and encourage them when they show an interest. No child is born with a taste for certain music or art or literature or drama. That taste will develop from what the child is exposed to. If you as a parent expose your children to the best, chances are they will develop a taste for the best; they will establish standards that demand more than simply titillation of the senses, and they will come to appreciate what a vast world of opportunities lies before them.

Of course, the worst thing we can do with our children is force them into anything, or try to live our dreams through them. If they decide to make magic or theater or sports or music a part of their lives, it should be because they decide to, not because their parents have pushed them into it. The love has to be there. Imposing an activity on an uninterested or unwilling child can be almost as damaging as ignoring the child; both extremes fail to acknowledge the child's worth as an individual and the unique attributes that make him or her special to us.

What a joy it is when we recognize the wonder of a God who has entrusted to mothers and fathers the development and growth of a human personality. How exciting, too, when we stop and think that to parents has been graciously given the opportunity of procreation. And that they will be models for what the new life was meant to be — a life of love, tenderness, and care.

When Ryan was nine months old, he was baptized. The beauty and wonder of baptism is that it is a time when we claim the grace of a God who loves our children and, indeed, gave them life, for every child is a never-to-be-repeated miracle of God. We also commit ourselves to help our children to grow in their faith. As Jesus said, "Let the little children come to me; do not stop them; for it is to such as these that the kingdom of God belongs" (Mark 10:14).

That morning we joined other parents and their children in prayer and asked God to pour out His power upon us as we committed ourselves to affirm our faith and to dedicate our homes to be places where our children would be raised in the love and care of the Lord. We asked the Holy Spirit to come upon us in a new way — that every word we might speak, every action we take, every reaction we communicate might be an extension of the Lord's love. It was an awesome promise.

Fortunately, our family is made stronger by the work of the Sunday school and the wider program of the church as well as the support and love of grandparents and other relations. In it all we believe there will be that glorious moment when our child will say, "What happened then at that day I now claim for myself."

"You baptized me," our three-year-old son told our pastor after viewing the videotape of that event.

"Yes, I did!" our pastor replied.

"You put water on my head."

"Yes, I did."

I cannot know if Ryan, even as an infant, felt the significance of that spiritual connection, but I like to think that, at some level, he did, and that the videotape awoke some preverbal memory of the love flowing from his parents, the pastor, the congregation, the Spirit itself. Certainly we all felt it.

And now, as Ryan grows and flourishes, we feel something else. "They grow up so quickly!" is the often heard refrain about children. And that's true, but to it I would add, "Yes, and so do the parents." While a great deal has been written about the nurturing and protecting of children, we continue, as I am sure many parents do, to rely upon our instincts, prayer, advice from close friends, and Scripture as well as our own experiences as children. What our parents did — or did not do — can guide us as we forge this most precious bond and fulfill this taxing yet rewarding responsibility.

At times, we adults wish in our hearts for a simpler, more peaceful time — a time when pleasures were pure and problems distant. A time of childhood innocence. A time when our imaginations were allowed to run free, unrestrained by the limitations and harsh realities forced upon us by adulthood. A time when possibilities were infinite. We can find that source of human contact and comfort by spending time with our children; in so doing we protect their innocence and, in many significant ways, get back in touch with our own.

I will be forever grateful to God for giving us a child, and to Patti for the way she has cared for us and herself as we continue to follow God's lead in raising and educating our son. Someday, should Ryan have his own family, I trust that he, too, will know that joy and that he will understand what we have come to understand: Nothing can be holier or more miraculous than to participate in the creation and maturation of new, innocent life.

CHAPTER FIVE

betrayal of trust

All things betray thee, who betrayest Me.

— Francis Thompson

O fficer, are you trying to tell us that our son is
dead?"

My father's words still haunt me thirty-five years after
he spoke them. He was seated at the kitchen table next
to my mother. A police officer sat on the opposite side.
The time was 2:00 A.M.

Unknown to any of them, I was huddled at the top
of the stairs, in my pajamas, watching and listening while
my younger brother slept in his bedroom down the hall.

Just moments before, I had been startled awake by the piercing ring of the doorbell. Peeking through my curtains, I saw a black-and-white police car parked in the driveway next to my parents' white Mustang. Then I heard the creak of my parents' bed and the rustle of clothing as my father got up and slipped on his trousers, followed by the concerned whispers of my mother as they crept downstairs, opened the front door, and led the officer to the kitchen. It felt surreal.

Oh, how I had wished this were only a movie from which I could exit! But it wasn't. Worse still, I knew why the officer had come, but my parents did not.

"Do you have a son?" he asked.

"Yes, we do," said my father, softly. My heart sank.

"Do you know where he is?"

"Yes, he's in bed, asleep."

There was a pause, then the officer said, "An hour ago I clocked a white Mustang at eighty miles per hour, racing side by side with another car."

Then my father interrupted to ask his question, the question I will always remember:

"Officer, are you trying to tell us that our son is dead?"

The time between that question and the officer's response must have seemed an eternity to my parents. In reality, only a moment passed. "No, fortunately, I'm not," he said.

As the officer explained, he had spotted us and written down the Mustang's license plate number while chasing and eventually catching the other driver. Then he traced the car to my house.

Centuries ago the Greek playwright Euripides called the death of a child the "grief surpassing all." In that split second with the officer, when my father had expressed his deepest fear, I believe my parents thought they had lost their elder son. That I caused that momentary shock pains me still — even though they have long since forgiven me and dismissed the incident entirely.

After the officer had left, my parents could have hugged me, said all was well, and sent me to bed with no further mention of the matter. Fortunately, for my own moral sense and our family's well-being, my parents have always believed in the importance of truth by confrontation, a principle they had learned from their own parents.

I can't begin to relate in words the shame I felt after the patrol car pulled away and I sat alone with them. I still marvel at the steadiness with which my father spoke. I can still see the disappointment and hurt in his eyes, and in my mother's. I can still hear the dismayed tone in his voice. I had dishonored them, but even more, I had hurt the very people who loved me the most.

I had betrayed their trust in me.

A mark of maturity and one of the most important lessons we can impart to our children (and claim and reclaim for ourselves as parents) is the capacity to perceive the consequences of our actions before we take them. From childhood episodes such as this, I learned that whenever I am about to do or say something that goes against my better judgment — MAGNIFY THE CON- SEQUENCES.

That night and in the incident's aftermath, for example, I wondered, *What if I had lost control of the car? What if I had hit the other car? What if...? What if...?* Fortunately, the story ended happily, and ever since I have been grateful for that moment of insight, for it also helped me to appreciate and understand the strength of my parents' connection to me. I elected never again to act in a way that devalued that.

The actions we take are often an extension of our thoughts, the manifestation of conscious choices. We choose to do something, or we choose not to. We can choose to be faithful to our mate, or not to. We can choose to be honest with our children, or not to. We can choose to keep a promise, or not to. As I like to remind my stu- dents, we were given a mind to serve us and to govern our behavior. If we cannot control our thoughts, we cannot control our lives.

As we have control of our thoughts, so (with obvious exceptions) we have control of our feelings. At any given moment, if I am feeling bored (about an event in my life), or angry (about a remark made by a friend), or bitter (about a rejection), or annoyed (about a relation) — I am creating those feelings. This is why Proverbs 4:23 is so adamant in saying, "Keep your heart with all vigilance, for from it flow the springs of life."

I was deeply moved by the emotional force of President Ronald Reagan's description of his father's alcoholism in his 1965 autobiography, *Where's the Rest of Me?* In a searing passage, Reagan recalls that when he was eleven he came home on a cold winter day to find his father "flat on his back on the front porch and no one there to lend a helping hand but me." Jack Reagan's arms were spread out "as if he were crucified — as indeed he was."

The young Reagan might have taunted his father or, even worse, ignored him and gone his own way, callous and embittered. Instead, the slender boy managed to drag his muscular father off the snowy porch and deposited him in bed. Even at such a tender age, and with every reason to resent the betrayal implicit in his father's actions, the boy chose instead to honor his parent by keeping quiet about the episode, thereby resisting the temptation to bring upon his father further shame. Reagan chose the emotion that guided his actions, opting for respect rather than rage. (Although some readers may be inclined to interpret this incident as an example of the well-known psychological principle of denial, I understand it as a choice of respect over rage. Reagan himself says he felt "no resentment" against his father. Instead, he felt himself "fill with grief" for him, and knew he had to accept responsibility. "If we don't accept it [and some don't]," he continues, "then we must just grow older without quite growing up." In his mind, too, was his mother Nelle's repeated message that "alcoholism was a sickness," and that they "should love and help our father and never condemn him for something that was beyond his control.")

In contrast, every day dozens of family members *choose* to betray loved ones by venting their venom in public confessions on the boggling array of television talk shows. Such disclosures and accusations may sell advertising spots, but they also violate the sanctity of the home as husbands and wives, hungry for their fifteen minutes of fame, spew abuse upon each other before a national audience, often with their own children sitting next to them. The widely distributed tabloids also exploit familial disruptions as couples or siblings or children break trust with those whose feelings they should be guarding the most carefully.

My pastor advised me long ago not to say anything about anyone that I wouldn't be willing to say to that person face-to-face twenty-four hours later. I have tried to follow that advice, and while at times it hasn't been easy, certainly it has helped me be more sensitive to the destructive, insidious effects of spreading petty resentments to others.

As husbands and wives, we must avoid the temptation to betray confidences or complain to others outside the home (with the exception, of course, of a professional counselor). Couples must be able to believe in each other, and in the gentle, careful manner in which a partner will receive and keep what we share. The richest relationships are those that allow us to reveal our true selves in all our vulnerability, and we cannot and will not do so unless we know that self will be safe. I would never gossip with others about my wife's family, for example, because to do so would violate her trust in me and undermine our relationship. It would also damage the interactions of the relatives and the person to whom I tell the tale.

As parents, we must also nurture the family's circle of trust. Now that I am a father of (at this writing) a twelve-year-old boy, I do my best to stay alert to how my actions or words might affect him. I don't want to risk weakening the respect that he has for me through any demonstration of disrespect toward him. My actions are still guided by the words of a trusted advisor, who told me years ago, "Be careful your son doesn't begin to doubt you." I have learned not to laugh at Ryan's fears, for to him they are real and threatening. I have learned to apologize when I have been impatient or unreasonable in my demands. And I have learned not to withhold my love and understanding. Parents who do may find their children turning elsewhere to satisfy unmet emotional needs.

On the other hand, a lack of parental discipline betrays the sense of security and safety that can come only from loving limits. Children need clear boundaries, and we let our kids down if we are too distracted or unconcerned to set them. Likewise, the ways we communicate and enforce those limits can affect a child deeply. Correcting children in front of others can make them feel ashamed. Referring to their mistakes as sins upsets their sense of values. Nagging or inconsistency only confuses them and makes them lose faith in us, as does ignoring or trivializing their questions. To a child, said psychologist Jean Piaget, no question is absurd. Children also need us to stay fit and healthy; failing to do so — when we have a *choice* to do so — is a betrayal of another kind, for illness can sap the whole family's resources and responding and attending to kids requires tremendous physical stamina.

It's hard work to be so mindful of the ramifications of our choices in our relationships, and sometimes family members simply fail to consider the consequences of their actions until it is too late. My friend Carla wishes her father had thought more about what effects his choices had.

"Together in the house, but miles apart": That is how she and her two sisters define their life together as children at home.

"It's as if our family had a subconscious agreement not to speak the truth," she told me one day. "Oh, we talked, but we were never honest with what was going on. Never direct about our feelings. Never said or showed anything about making and keeping commitments. I feel the lack even today, but I've sworn to myself that as long as I live I'll do everything in my power to prevent my own children from having a childhood like mine."

When Carla turned nine, her parents divorced. "It was over so quickly, but we weren't surprised," she said. "The signs had been there for a long time — the arguments, the shouting, the slamming doors, the retreats into silence. Day in. Day out. Year in. Year out. All this seeped into my soul. One day Daddy just took each of us aside and said he was going to live somewhere else now, but that we would still be able to see him."

None of the children saw him leave, however, and concluded that he must have done so while they were at school. "Just like that," she said. "He was gone. The utter emptiness I felt at the time I can't begin to describe. It was horrible."

One of the most visible signs of our increasing separateness and, in its turn, the cause of ever greater separation, is divorce. Sometimes, granted, it is unavoidable. Sometimes we fail. Jesus himself explains that divorce was allowed in the Mosaic Law because of the hard-heartedness of people.

But all too often parents who decide to part have not fully considered the impact their choice will have on their children, for whom such a schism is always confusing and frightening. They fail to magnify the consequences, to envision what their actions can look like through the eyes of their children. Divorce represents, as both Stephen L. Carter and Margaret Farley have pointed out, "the sundering of the very union that brought the children themselves into existence." In Carla's case, unfortunately, that sundering took an even more tragic turn.

Nine years later, Carla's father died from a self-inflicted gunshot — a mere two weeks after he had invited all of his daughters to see him for Easter weekend. "I think he knew it was the last visit," she said. "For the first time in our life, he took us to a sunrise service at the beach. We spent the morning together. We hugged. I never saw him alive again."

Carla remembers being in her university dormitory room, alone, when her mother called to say that "Daddy had died" and that she would talk to her later to tell her the circumstances. Because it was morning, and everyone was at class, my friend had no one to talk to until late afternoon when her fiancé returned to his room.

"He was my comfort and my rock during those awful first days," she said. "He stayed with me the rest of the evening, and stayed by me when I called my mother to find out how it happened." She described the conversation:

"My mother used few words and said she didn't know why Daddy did it. He had gone to work that morning but had not returned home for dinner. Mary, his current wife, went to his office, a small house that had been redone, and found that he had shot himself in the head. Mom asked me if I had anyone there with me, but she offered no other words of comfort. I don't really know, but I suspected that she was angry that Daddy had done this and left her the awful chore of notifying other family members and friends, planning a funeral, mourning him, and everything else."

"Could the divorce have caused this?" I asked.

"I doubt it. There was a lot more. I believe that all his difficulties in life — he had gone into business for himself as a landscape architect, but was not doing well — merely precipitated the suicide. They did not cause it. But still, none of us children could understand it. We still can't. That's what's so bad about suicide."

She was eighteen then, confused and deeply saddened. She felt betrayed by the very individual she ought most to trust in — her father.

"We were left with guilt and anger, with sifting through good memories and bad, and trying to understand something that is awful beyond expression. No chance to reconcile, to say good-bye.

"And then there's the corrosive presence of guilt," she added. "All the things done and left undone: the arguments, the slights, the unreturned telephone calls, the doctor not notified, the psychiatric hospitalization postponed or resisted."

For Carla, the only consolation, if that is the word for it, is that when a fellow employee at work came to her for help, she was able to offer it. Her friend's ex-husband was stalking her, and she said she was close to killing herself. Carla begged her friend to reconsider, explaining that her children would never understand. They made plans for her friend to leave the state for a safe haven, and when she returned her job would be waiting for her.

"Perhaps," Carla says, "that's why God put me there at that job."

Others came forward to commiserate with Carla. A high school acquaintance revealed that her father had also taken his own life, and she thought it was a truly selfish act. She was filled with anger, not sorrow. It helped Carla to realize that her own reactions were not unique. Eventually, a renewed appreciation for the preciousness of life emerged from this experience, along with a cautiousness about signs within herself of the depression or temptation that had caused her father's final act. And although Carla's life is now contented with much love, success, and friendship, she knows from a hard, hard teacher that these are not always enough to counter the pain and destructiveness of what she later suspected to be her father's severe mental illness, and so the possibility of suicide is a recurring presence in her own mind.

As English historian Arnold Toynbee wrote in *Man's Concern with Death*, "There are two parties to the suffering that death inflicts; and, in the apportionment of this suffering, the survivor takes the brunt." The intentional ending of one's own life exacerbates that suffering exponentially, for it represents the violent, chosen sundering of connections, the very negation of relationships and trust. Suicide, in a sense, murders love. As one of the characters says in Arthur Miller's *After the Fall*, "A suicide kills two people, Maggie, that's what it's for!"

Each year thirty thousand Americans commit suicide. That's almost one person every seventeen minutes or more than seventy persons a day. Another half million attempt it seriously enough to require medical treatment. The reasons for suicide and means for its prevention are the subjects of several brilliant books, including A. Alvarez's *The Savage God: A Study of Suicide* and Kay Redfield Jamison's *Night Falls Fast: Understanding Suicide,* among others. My point is that, as the ultimate betrayal of trust, suicide can have mind-numbing, soul-shattering effects upon the family, particularly young children.

"Suicide is a death like no other," writes Jamison, "and those who are left behind to struggle with it must confront a pain like no other. They are left with the shock and the unending 'what ifs.'

"Most of all," Jamison continues, "they are left to miss a parent or child whose life was threaded to theirs from its very beginning, mourn a spouse whose bed and love and trust they shared, or grieve the loss of a confidant with whom they spent long days and evenings of friendship."

Choosing to end one's life is one way of dealing with great pain. It is, of course, an extreme reaction, for many of us live with and through great suffering. Unfortunately, all too often that suffering is inflicted, directly or indirectly, by the very people God entrusted with our care — parents and grandparents, spouses, and other family members. Many have betrayed that trust; and, as a result, the degree to which so many people have grown disconnected

from themselves and from one another is both sad and dis-
turbing.

Over the past twenty-seven years I have taught a class
called Literature of the Bible. Among the many questions
I ask my students on their final examination, the following is one of my (and their) favorites: "Name a character
from either the Old or New Testament (exception: Jesus)
with whom you identify in some particular way. You may
focus on life pattern, personality, conflicts faced, tests
endured, or anything else that helps you to explain as
specifically as possible that identification."

It may not come as a surprise when I say that, of the
hundreds of characters they could choose from, at least
one-third of the students identify with Job because, they
say, he too suffered without cause. His dilemma is an
ancient and primeval one. How can we reconcile human
suffering, especially the suffering of the innocent, with
the existence of an omnipotent God of justice and love?

Until I began to teach at the college level I don't think
I had realized just how many students come from tormented homes that are filled with anger, shouting, and
abuse; homes in which children are trained with less love
and patience than you'd use with a puppy; homes in
which children come away without any words of affirmation or any of the blessings that are so necessary for their
nurturing and well-being. This is a betrayal of the most
lasting kind. One twenty-year-old student, for example,
wrote the following:

> Job experienced the dark night of the soul.
> So have I. He suffered from depression. So
> have I. He had foolish friends. So have I.
> He cried out for God's help. So have I. He
> remained strong and, by God's grace,
> pulled through in the end. So have I.

When asked, she was not at all hesitant to say that her parents betrayed her. Yes, she had a home, enough food and money, early education, and a stay-at-home mother who raised three girls. Yes, her father was a successful businessman. "He did have breakfast with us every Sunday and we were able to see him read the newspaper," she said. "As soon as breakfast was over, my father continued to read the paper." But that did not bother her. At least she was able to see him. But this pleasant exterior was deceiving, for beneath it was a cauldron of tension and abuse.

"All I ever wanted," she said, "was to be in a family like *The Brady Bunch* or *Family Ties*. Instead, I had an alcoholic father who ignored us and a controlling mother who was overly critical of me."

From as far back as my student can remember, her parents had problems, but these escalated when she turned fifteen. She wrote:

> They fought about everything. As their
> problems escalated, the name calling and
> screaming increased. At first they argued

about money. Then they began to argue
about their failures as an adequate spouse.
Then they began to argue about who was
at fault for *my* failures. I was then no
longer their child, but their battleground.
I began to feel that my failures were the
cause of the family breakup.

When she was nineteen, her parents refused to help
pay for her education. So she dropped out of college,
moved in with her boyfriend, and found a job. Although
she was intelligent and had the potential of being a good
student, she was too busy drinking and nightclubbing
every night of the week in an attempt to ease her depression. But after her boyfriend started hitting her and
threatening to make her life worse, she decided that she
had had enough and moved back home. She explained,

My parents never realized that I was
rebelling because I was depressed. I could
not handle my life. I hated living. I was
ready to die. I no longer wanted anything.
I did not want to go to school or have a
family. I had no dreams, plans, or goals.
All I wanted to do was drink myself to
death or jump off a building. I felt that
because of my problems, I was solely
responsible for my parents' fights.

She said that her parents hated each other and didn't care that they were tearing apart the family. But they never divorced. They just stopped talking to one another and moved to opposite sides of the house. They argued all the time, but they never left. Nor did they attempt to repair the family. "They just seemed to disappear into their own hatred," she explained, "and they became blind to my depression and suicidal thoughts." Along with that, her middle sister grew aggressive and angry, and her younger sister receded beyond anyone's reach into her own depression. She wrote:

> My parents would say that they did their best to raise us, and perhaps this is true. My parents also would say that their marital problems had nothing to do with us, and consequently their problems did not affect us. My parents believed that their arguments did not hurt us psychologically. They believed that even when they were screaming at each other, they were not hurting us. They believed that we were old enough to handle all the chaos they created in our home.
>
> But they were wrong. My parents failed us. They and all other parents who fight and argue with each other are wrong. It hurts me when one insults the other. It

hurts me when they blame each other for my mistakes rather than asking me how they could help. It hurt me when they destroyed our family.

When my student turned twenty-one, she seriously considered attempting suicide by driving her car off a freeway ramp. To this day she knows it was only by the grace of God that she decided she had to do something, and so she went to a psychologist for help. But during the first session, she became enraged when he told her that because she was still living at home she was a failure at independent living. "I walked out. I had had enough. I was no longer going to be destroyed by my parents. I am not a failure and I was not going to be labeled like that by anyone, not by my parents, friend, society, or a psychologist."

After she made that decision, for the first time in a long time, she felt strong. She felt she could live through this. With the help of her sisters, she moved out and worked to build a new "family" among the three of them. She grew up and vowed that never again would she allow anger or depression to control her. She was as emotionally supportive of her sisters as she could be. She began to have dreams and set goals again. She returned to college — and that was when I met her.

"My parents cannot take credit for this change," she told me one day in my office. "I accomplished this on my own. I found the strength within myself. Yes, I am what I am because of my parents. But if I stay that way, I'm to blame." She described the turning point:

> One day my parents were screaming at each other again. One threatened divorce. There was fighting, broken glasses, slammed doors.
>
> "Stop!" I screamed repeatedly. "I can't take this anymore!"
>
> They were screaming the most awful things imaginable to each other. I felt like something inside of me was tearing apart. I could no longer take another minute. I could not take the screaming. I could not take the name-calling. I could not take the abuse they inflicted upon each other. I got up off the couch, grabbed my keys, and ran out of the door. They did not even flinch.
>
> As I ran out, they continued to yell at each other. I turned on the car and took off. I did not know where I was going. I did not know what I was going to do. My hands were shaking. I needed a cigarette. I lit one as I was driving away. I could not see the road ahead of me because my eyes were full of tears. I continued driving and smoking.
>
> A twenty-one-year-old is not supposed

to cry over her parents arguing. I should
have been used to this by now. However, I
was not and it still hurt. I refused to surrender to my despair.

At that moment, with that insight, my student's sense of
helplessness and unworthiness began to lift. Although her
parents continue to have hatred within their hearts,
although they continue to find fault within each other, she
and her sisters now no longer blame them for the failures in
their lives. Instead, they have forgiven them and moved on.

"I have learned a lot from my experiences," she told me
recently. "I have learned it is possible to forgive but not to
trust. And I now believe that the foundation of anyone's
life is a family. When parents fail at providing a loving,
supportive family life for their child, nothing else matters."
Then she quoted a passage from Mitch Albom's book,
Tuesdays with Morrie: "The fact is, there is no foundation,
no secure ground, upon which people may stand today if
it isn't the family. . . . Love is so supremely important."

As our great poet W. H. Auden once said, "We must
love one another or die."

Some philosophers claim that suicide is the ultimate
betrayal of the trust of loved ones. But infidelity, abuse,
drug addiction, and alcoholism are also dreadful assaults

on the underpinnings of a family. Such destructive behaviors all point to a similar dilemma, one that novelist Leo Tolstoy identified when he said that at times we live in defiant opposition to the dictates of our conscience and our common sense.

In writing to the Romans, Paul similarly describes two warring forces within his own mind: "I do not understand my own actions. For I do not do what I want, but I do the very thing I hate....I can will what is right, but I cannot do it" (7:15, 18). Johann Wolfgang von Goethe echoes the sentiment when he has Faust say, "Two souls, alas, are dueling in my breast." And in *Dr. Jekyll and Mr. Hyde,* Robert Louis Stevenson describes an individual who is swayed one moment by the beneficent Dr. Jekyll in his nature, and the next by his evil and murderous Mr. Hyde nature. Psychiatrist Carl Jung, who likened the defiant part of us to the wild, ravenous wolf, wrote that this conflict may be between "the sensual and the spiritual."

Others have referred to these two inner forces as the "life instinct" and "death instinct." One seeks to preserve life, the other seeks to destroy it. People standing near the edge of a deep canyon, for example, often sense an inner agent that toys, if ever so briefly, with the notion of jumping over the edge. But they also sense and heed another agent that causes them to step back. I recall as a child sitting in the backseat of our car as we sped along the tollway, and sometimes lifting the door handle ever so slightly, to see how far I could raise it without opening the door. Fortunately, I never did, but I was yielding to that urge to approach the precipice, nonetheless.

How can we learn to recognize and reduce these opposing forces and the destructive effects they may have on those around us?

In 2 Corinthians 12:9 we find assurance that in our weakness, God's "grace is sufficient," and that grace should be our hope when life becomes intolerable. When nothing we try works, God has promised that He is able to sustain us. In his letter to the Romans, Paul himself answered the question he had raised:

> Who will rescue me from this body of death? I thank God there is a way out through Jesus Christ our Lord....While Christ was actually taking upon Himself the sins of men, God condemned that sinful nature. So that...we are living no longer by the dictates of our sinful nature, but in obedience to the promptings of the Spirit....Now if Christ does live within you His presence means that your sinful nature is dead. (7:25; 8:3–4, 10, NASV)

Trust in that promise gives us the inner strength to earn, treasure, and keep the trust of others. When we learn to rely on the promptings of the Spirit, we will always act in a way that allows those we love to rely on us.

the family of god

---

*My religion is summed up in the first two words
of the Lord's Prayer: "Our Father."*

— OLIVER WENDELL HOLMES, JR.

One evening in May 1969, my friend Jerry was sitting
alone in his car on the Purdue University campus,
where he was a senior and soon to graduate. It was 11:00
P.M. He had just returned from a Bible study in one of
the fraternity houses, that he had agreed to attend with
the student body pastor. In the midst of the songs, the
fellowship, and the lesson, it had become clear to Jerry
that the thirty students gathered there had something
that he did not. What was it? A depth of feeling. A

connectedness. A certainty. An inner peace that showed itself on their faces, in their gestures, in their attitudes.

This had come to him as a surprise: He had *thought* he was contented! After all, he had been raised by solid, sensible parents. He never doubted their love. Or their devotion. Or their trust. He had loyal friends. He enjoyed his coursework and eagerly looked forward to graduate school next fall. He went to church most Sundays, believed in and trusted God, and prayed every day. And yet...

After the Bible study, and over coffee, he had related to the pastor that sometimes late at night he would stand in the driveway outside his home and look up, with arms outstretched, wishing to be held close. Many nights he fell asleep in bed with his Bible clutched tightly to his chest. Deep within him, he knew, all was not well. There was a hidden core of loneliness, even despair at times, that neither his loving parents, his challenging classes, nor his promising future could touch.

"My faith is strong," he told the pastor. "I know *about* God. But something someone said earlier this evening has shown me that I don't *know* God in my personal experience."

Now, for Jerry to admit this was very hard. Usually he would feel slightly embarrassed, even awkward. But in this instance, he was relaxed, encouraged to speak without fear of ridicule, without a need for self-editing. He spoke as he wanted and needed to do, and that was refreshing.

In response, the pastor quoted from St. Augustine's

Confessions: "Thou hast made us for Thyself and our hearts are restless till they rest in Thee." Then with patience and tenderness he led Jerry through the Scriptures in a way he had never heard before, identifying with his yearning, urging him forward in his quest.

As the pastor explained, all of us long for the touch of God the Father. God wants us to obey Him and to live with Him. But we have broken with God. We have neither obeyed Him nor loved Him, and out of pride or guilt or fear we have fled from His Presence. God's work in redemption is to undo the tragic effects of that revolt, to bring us back again into the right and eternal relationship with Himself.

"That is what you're feeling," he said, "a yearning to return to the Father."

"How?" Jerry asked.

"By submitting," he said. "You can't earn His love. You can do nothing to deserve it. All you can do is humbly submit all of yourself, confess — and ask for His forgiveness and mercy, as would a child. God doesn't want our performance. He wants our heart."

And so, alone in his car Jerry prayed the words that he had heard others pray many times, that he had read in countless places, but that seemed now to be his and his alone: "Dear Lord, forgive me for my sins. I want to *know* you personally, and I give you my life. Open my eyes so that I may see. Come into my heart."

Before he had even finished speaking, a rush of peace

and ineffable joy filled his entire body. He felt washed clean and full of an immense energy. With absolute certainty he knew in that instant the palpable embrace of a loving Father. And in the midst of his uncontrollable sobs of joy, he cried over and over, "Thank you, Heavenly Father. Thank you!"

Never had he been so certain of anything. He *knew:* Beyond all doubt!

Upon returning home, Jerry opened his Bible to the Gospel of John, and read. This time these familiar words became more than little black marks on the page; these familiar stories became more than stories from the distant past. As if he were seeing them for the first time in his life, certain verses leaped off the page, flooding his interior being and opening up deep sources of illumination:

> But to all who received him, who believed
> in his name, he gave power to
> become children of God. (1:12)
> Very truly, I tell you, no one can see the
> Kingdom of God without being
> born from above [anew]. (3:3)
> For God so loved the world that he gave his
> only Son, so that everyone who
> believes in him may not perish but
> have eternal life. (3:16)
> Indeed, just as the Father raises the dead

and gives them life, so also the Son
gives life to whomever he wishes.
(5:21)
I am the light of the world. Whoever follows
me will never walk in darkness but
will have the light of life. (8:12)
The Father and I are one. (10:30)
Whoever serves me must follow me, and
where I am, there will my servant
be also. Whoever serves me, the
Father will honor. (12:26)
I am the way, and the truth, and the life.
No one comes to the Father except
through me. (14:6)
You did not choose me but I chose you.
And I appointed you to go and bear
fruit, fruit that will last, so that the
Father will give you whatever you
ask him in my name. (15:16)
Blessed are those who have not seen and
yet have come to believe. (20:29)

These words and others spoke as if written just for
him — a personal letter from his Father. They seemed to
say, "Welcome, my son."

When we experience in ourselves the transforming
power and fullness of God's presence, our relationships

with others will be transformed as well. Given the busy-ness of our lives, the burdens and the pressures of caring for a family, it is easy for husbands and wives, children and parents to drift apart so slowly and subtly that no one notices the change until the chasm is too wide to bridge. That evening, Jerry felt a mounting desire to close that space, to reach out and care for others — family, friends, even strangers. He had broken through a shell of safety, of self-centeredness that he had been unaware he'd built, and felt a loving responsibility for others. Filled with joy, he fell asleep with a peace that he'd never known existed.

The next morning Jerry awoke and everything seemed different: cleaner, crisper, newer, as if he had been for-given an enormous debt, the accumulation of a lifetime of separation and alienation. And he knew that he wanted to deepen his intimacy with God, but that he could only do that by continuing to submit, totally and irrevocably, to His will. He also knew it would not be easy.

Now when he recalls that turning point — as he often does — there is in his mind a picture of being lost on a moonless night, but not knowing that he was lost; and of seeing a big house on the hill with light at all its windows and the sound of music as he neared. There was the assur-ance that inside the big house were food and warmth and the gladsome singing of hymns, and he would be wel-comed. That night he had moved from *believing* to *know-ing:* There is a huge difference.

Although over the years Jerry has shared his momentous experience with many people of many faiths and some with no faith at all, never has he questioned their own beliefs or religion. As he said to me one day, "I can only live by and share the Truth as I know it. What I received was a gift, unearned and undeserved. On matters concerning God, I am in no position to judge others, but only to learn from them." Ultimately, only God knows the truth of another's heart.

Moments like Jerry's do not come out of nowhere. What happened to him was the accumulation, I believe, of twenty-one years of inner struggles that blossomed into a sudden sense of who he was and what he needed to be. All that time, God had been waiting to embrace him, to know him, and to love him. His Spirit had been preparing Jerry's heart: softening here, suggesting there, nudging here, until an "inner must" grew to be so strong that he could turn nowhere else but to Him. It was entirely God's doing. "The wind blows where it chooses," we are told in the Gospel of John; "and you hear the sound of it, but you do not know where it comes from or where it goes. So it is with everyone who is born of the Spirit" (3:8). For the breath of that Spirit flowing over and into him, Jerry is eternally thankful.

Different traditions have different names for this experience, but I understand it to be *grace* — God's unmerited favor.

Since Jerry's experience that evening in his car, God has become the center of his life. He knows that God is his personal creator, and that the breath of his Maker is always within him. All of his abilities, whatever they might be, are, he believes, gifts of God. And when misfortune has entered his life, as it inevitably does, he accepts it as the working out of the divine will, in which he acquiesces without grumbling; and in his times of trouble he feels comfort and support. These beliefs have become the foundations on which Jerry has built his life — and his family's!

As I reread what I have written, I am reminded of a scene from my childhood. On Saturday mornings I loved going to the clothing store and, as my mother or father shopped, darting gently among the hanging clothes.

One day, to my horror, the lights went off and I found that I was lost in a confusion of hanging slacks, shirts, and coats. Nowhere could I find my father. In panic, I yelled, "Daddy! Daddy!"

From a distance, I heard, "Over here, Dale. I'm over here!"

I inched my way toward the source, the voice growing louder, until suddenly I felt a hand, which I recognized as my father's, push through the clothing. I held onto it and he pulled me close to his side just as the lights were restored.

What I have learned is that, in like manner, our Heavenly Father extends His hand to guide us out of the confusion of our lives into the light of His truth. "Trust in the Lord with all your heart, and do not rely on your own insight," says Proverbs. "In all your ways acknowledge him, and he will make straight your paths" (3:6).

I think now of Walter Miller, whom I first met on an autumn day in 1991 as students arrived for my Literature of the Bible class. In he walked, a man in his sixties who seemed much younger, with a bright, intelligent face, full of candor, full of good sense; and his smile was a smile of frank, undisguised friendship — with just a hint of mischief. He settled his six-foot four-inch frame in the back row — "the back of the choir" as I like to call it — and over the next few weeks brought to our discussions thoughtful answers and insightful questions. Here was the voice of a modest man.

But nothing moved me or the class more, than when he shared with us one of the great sorrows of his life after we had finished a study of the Book of Job.

For years his dream had been to have a healthy son with whom he could figuratively grow up again. That dream was fulfilled on Friday, April 13, 1945, when his wife presented him with a baby boy.

On October 10, 1948, that dream ended. His son — only three and a half years old — died in the hospital from the torment of polio.

No one can ever be ready for such a blow, but Walter could not have been less prepared.

"This isn't the way life is supposed to work," he said to the class. "Our children are supposed to survive us, to go on with the family name and fulfill all their potential. But my son didn't even have a chance."

At the time of his son's death, Walter told us, he was filled with anger. While some others around him could find a measure of solace in their faith, he had no such resource. "I hated God, even though I didn't know Him!" he explained.

He turned his back on his beautiful wife, who had just given birth to their second child. Over the next several weeks he lost interest in everyone and everything: his work, his home, his friends who tried to help. And he felt helpless and utterly alone. He had never hurt so badly.

He couldn't even look at their new baby.

Why did this have to happen — and to me? he wondered. Was this an example of God's love?

"I didn't know God at that time," Walter explained, "and I didn't want to! I was angry, and I was confused, and I was very hurt."

Then one day he received a call from the City of Hope Cancer Center in Duarte, California. A patient by the name of Dr. Elton Trueblood, a well-known writer and theologian, was dying from cancer. He wanted to see Walter.

"So I went to him," Walter said. "Not out of compassion — I was still trying to punish someone for the loss of my boy! — but because in my grief I knew I had to find some help."

Walter will never forget Dr. Trueblood's opening words: "Mr. Miller, you are so kind to visit me. I have heard about your terrible loss and what has happened since your son's death, and I have prayed someone, possibly you, could give me an answer to a question that has bothered me all my life."

This was a complete surprise to Walter. "I came to find answers, not give them!" he said pointedly.

"Why are you so bitter?" asked Dr. Trueblood. "From what I have been told, you are an educated man. How can you react this way?"

Walter remained standing before the bed, silent and scowling. All he wanted to do was leave.

Softly but firmly, Dr. Trueblood probed for the source of Walter's suffering. "Why do you think your son lived? Why did he die? Do you think the merciful God whom I and millions of others worship could be other than completely loving? Have you thought of Heaven? What kind of place would Heaven be if there were nothing but old folks there? Who really was and is your son's father? Could that little boy have lived and died so that you could come to know your Heavenly Father better than you do? Please help me understand."

Dr. Trueblood's words and the manner in which he delivered them were having an effect. Though he had spoken softly, his questions had roared. Walter could feel something warm rise within him, and for the first time since his son's death, he began to cry. Then he left the room.

Walter never saw Dr. Trueblood again, but that day, in December 1948, Walter's life changed direction. Out of the teeth of sorrow, he started to think and act differently. It wasn't easy, but he began to accept his son's death. Not exactly as Dr. Trueblood would have liked, perhaps, but he ceased being angry. He started paying attention to his wife; his lovely daughter, Rachel; his family; his job; and his friends, all of whom had tried so hard to help.

"I missed my son," he said, "and without shame I cried now and then when no one could see." But Scripture never condemns grief. In many stories, tears are valuable. They are God given. Even Jesus wept.

"I guess I was what you would call a *hard case*," Walter added, "because it was not until twenty years later that I really found the answers I was searching for. That was when I submitted to the Lord and prayed. That was when I joined God's family."

And, he added, "My son and I will see each other again! And Dr. Trueblood will be there, too."

We can sense many truths in Walter's story, but the one I want to hold up is this: We are God's children. He created us. He yearns to pull us close to Him. Never were we meant to go through life alone like orphans. To know a God who is so vitally interested in all His children's concerns is to have the secret of a peace, poise, and steadiness that nothing can disturb. Then we can pass out of the bondage of fear and grief. No longer do we depend on circumstances. Now we depend on God — for everything — while trusting, along with the Psalmist: "Weeping may linger for the night, but joy comes with the morning" (30:5).

My maternal grandmother used to say, "One of the worst things that happens to you as you grow old is that you start to bury your loved ones." To her, life was a series of good-byes — starting with a miscarriage, at seven months, caused by a fall from a stepladder while washing a ceiling; then later her own parents; her only son, Raymond, at sixty; and, inevitably, many, many friends.

Of course, my grandparents were from an era in which, when death came, it was the family that dealt with it, not the specialists, and in the home, not in the hospital. As

Ronald Blythe recalls, children were born and parents died in the same bed. It was a time "when the entire intimacy of life from start to finish was confined to the family house, and not to maternity wards, ending-up wards and funeral parlors."

But what sustained her above all, she said, was a glorious faith that she would see all of them again, something she thought of every Sunday afternoon, when it was the family custom to pilgrimage to the local cemetery with flowers. She believed that the connections we establish in life transcend even death itself. She accepted each death as the will of the Father, and tried to learn from the experience.

In many religions, divine compassion and love are expressed by the relationship of parent and child. In the Lotus Sutra, the Buddha is called Father of the World. Similar statements are found in the Vedas and the Confucian classics. Judaism and Christianity are unique, however, in their concept of a God who seeks a *personal* relationship with us.

In Scripture, the word for "Father" (in Aramaic: *Abba)* appears more than 150 times in the New Testament and a couple of dozen times in the Old. The word connotes intimacy, trust, warmth, tenderness, love — somewhat like the affectionate word "Daddy" that we use today. For behind all that God does is a loving heart constantly caring for His people, planning for them, watching over them — in times of joy, in times of loss. "If you then…know how to give good gifts to your children, how much more will your Father in heaven give good things to those who ask him!" (Matt. 7:11). We may approach Him without fear, and always be assured of His fatherly concern and care.

One of the earliest biblical references to God as Father appears in the Book of Exodus. Moses says to the Pharaoh, "Thus says the Lord: Israel is my firstborn son. I said to you, 'Let my son go'" (Exod. 4:22–3). In 2 Samuel 7:14, the Lord speaks of Himself as a father of the future king of Israel, Solomon: "I will be a father to him, and he shall be a son to me." In Psalm 68:5, David refers to God more personally as "Father of the orphans and protector of widows." In Psalm 103:13, he writes, "As a father has compassion for his children, so the Lord has compassion for those who fear him." And in Malachi 2:10, the prophet asks, "Have we not all one father? Has not one God created us?"

The Fatherhood of God is central to Jesus' teaching. Luke 2:49 gives us the first recorded words of the twelve-year-old Jesus who has wandered off from his parents: "Did you not know that I must be in my Father's house?" Some of the Old Testament writers had discerned God's relationship to us in terms of a potter and his clay, a creator and his creatures, a dictator and his subjects, or a covenant with the nation of Israel as a whole, not God as the Father of each individual Israelite. But these are impersonal images. According to Jesus, God's relationship to us is most like the family relationship of parent and child, and the Master used this analogy many times to illustrate his teachings. In Jesus' life, we see the perfect sonship, in which all the tenderness, strength, serenity, and security of Father-God are mirrored. Even at the culminating moment on the cross, when he cries in Mark 15:34, "My God, my God, why have you forsaken me?" — he follows with confidence, "Into your hands I commend my spirit" (Luke. 23:46). Jesus gave the word Father a new depth.

Just as a father loves each child in particular, God knows and loves each soul. Matthew writes, "And even the hairs of your head are all counted" (10:30). Like the shepherd who leaves the ninety-nine sheep and goes after the one stray, so does God the Father search for His lost children. As St. Augustine wrote, "He loves us every one as though there were but one of us to love." That He gave His only son to redeem the world is the ultimate sign of His love for the individual.

When we call God "Father," sin and forgiveness take on a new light. Sin becomes darker, for now we are not sinning against an impersonal law or abstract concept, but against a Father, against One who loves us. How much worse it is to behave in a way that injures a loving heart!

The interior journey of the soul from rebellion to the Presence of God the Father is beautifully illustrated in Luke's telling of the parable of the Prodigal Son. A man had two sons, the younger of whom took his inheritance, left his native land, and squandered his wealth recklessly. When he had nothing left, he saw himself as he was and said, "I will get up and go to my father, and I will say to him, 'Father, I have sinned against heaven and before you; I am no longer worthy to be called your son; treat me like one of your hired hands'" (15:18–19). When the son returned to his father, however, he was welcomed, embraced, kissed, and given a celebration. He had entered into the presence of his father.

In this parable, Jesus pictures God neither condemning His shamed child when he finally abandons his wicked ways, nor standing on His dignity when he comes home, but running out to gather him into His welcoming arms. The son could not outrun the love of his father, which remained steadfast even when the youth turned his back on home and family. Just so, we cannot outrun the love of our Heavenly Father.

Oftentimes our picture of God is cast in the image of our earthly father. I believe many of us are able to embrace the idea of God as Father in part because of our healthy relationships with our own fathers. But what about those who come from abusive relationships? For them accepting God's love can sometimes be difficult.

For years one of my colleagues had trouble trusting in the authority and loving nature of God because he had been abused by his authoritative father. For awhile as a high school student he immersed himself in his studies and sought distractions in his job. When those failed to satisfy him, he escaped into an ever increasing search for pleasure. Alcohol and drugs entered the picture. He dropped out of school. He married and divorced. He lost his friends. He lost his way.

But many nights, as he skulked back home, drunk and barely able to stand, and slipped upstairs to his bedroom, he could hear in his mind the echo of his grandmother's concerned voice from his childhood, saying, "I'm praying for you!"

Then his father died, followed shortly afterward by his mother. As much as he hated his father, he felt cheated, bereft. "One's father dies only once," he said, "and I missed it. I never had a chance to talk with him one last time." For a year or so afterward, my colleague says, he was visited by a recurring dream.

He sees himself in a retreat center (called "Cease"), sitting on a couch and saying to a student: "I want wholeness. I feel fragmented." Fellow students join in to listen, then offer their own thoughts.

A young woman, sitting to his right, turns to him and says, "All you need is to be loved." To his left, in a roped-off area, he sees his parents and brother, and he feels slightly embarrassed that they are there. He begins to weep and wishes this episode were occurring in private.

Now, he is seated in a chair, surrounded by students working from their textbooks. As each student completes a problem, he closes the text and looks up. Someone mentions the word "father," and again he weeps. The young woman to his right is now reading from a book entitled *The Yellow Book*. He leans forward in an attempt to read the words, but can't see the pages. Instead, he hears chimed music coming from her ear, and he realizes she is wearing a hearing aid.

Other students bring him elaborate floral cards as an offering of love; he tries to read the messages, but they are passing by him too quickly. Once again, he tries to read the words from *The Yellow Book* but he doesn't want to ignore the others caring for him. He feels like a child, and wonders about the sincerity of his outreaching peers. Are they just going through the motions, or are they genuinely concerned? Then he awakens.

"The supreme happiness of life is the conviction that we are loved," wrote the French novelist Victor Hugo. My friend's dream illustrates that. This longing extends further and deeper than any love humans can extend to us. He had to accept the love offered by others and trust that

God had the best for him in mind. He couldn't read the words inscribed in *The Yellow Book,* yet they were there, just as the Psalmist promised:

> Thou knowest me right well;
> my frame was not hidden from thee,
> when I was being made in secret,
> intricately woven in the depths of the earth.
> Thy eyes beheld my unformed substance;
> in thy book were written, every one of them,
> the days that were formed for me,
> when as yet there was none of them.
>
> (139:14–16, RSV)

The dream helped bring my colleague to himself. He began to attend church, to study the Scriptures, and respond slowly to the outreaching love of God. To meet him today, one would never guess the truth of his past, how close he came to giving up on life altogether.

"The greatest suffering," wrote Mother Teresa, "is being lonely, feeling unloved, just loving no one." To those who say, "My father disappointed me greatly," Scripture replies, "But praise God, my heavenly Father will be very different." To those who say, "I have never known what it is to have a father on earth," Scripture replies, "But praise God I now have one in heaven." To those who say, "I hate my father," Scripture replies, "But God loves you." Our relationship with God as our Father transcends the categories of human experience.

Paul tells us in his letter to the Ephesians that long before God laid down earth's foundation, in eternity past, He had us in mind, having settled on us as the focus of his love, "to be holy and blameless before him in love" (1:4). He created us without our help, St. Augustine reminds us, and loved us without our deserving it. And because He created us, God has the right to claim us as His children, to adopt us into His family through Jesus Christ.

Ultimately, we are never alone. Verse after verse beautifully assures us of the closeness of God and His protective providence among His children. Paul says to the Athenians, God "is not far from each one of us. For 'In him we live and move and have our being.'" (Acts 17:27–8). When the prophet Jeremiah fears the mission God wants for him, God encourages and consoles him: "Do not be afraid,…for I am with you to deliver you" (1:8). Joshua is reassured: "Be strong and courageous; do not be frightened or dismayed, for the Lord your God is with you wherever you go" (1:9). And the last words of Christ to his apostles: "I am with you always, to the end of the age" (Matt. 28:20).

Yes, it is terrible to be lonely, to feel unloved, to lack the touch of loving parents. But how much worse it is to go through life without ever realizing the purpose for which we were born: to know the love of God. Nothing is more important. When we reach the end of our lifetime, we can embrace the Father, as Henri J. M. Nouwen counsels the dying, as if we are a trapeze artist. "Dying is trusting in the catcher," he wrote. "To care for the dying is to say, 'Don't be afraid. Remember that you are the beloved child of God. He will be there when you make your long jump. Don't try to grab him; he will grab you. Just stretch out your arms and hands and trust, trust, trust.'"

the gift of love

Love has no meaning if it isn't shared.

— MOTHER TERESA

*I*n my mind I hold an image: of a hospital patient, pale and thin, lying under a single sheet, eyes open and clear, speaking in the tone of a child and so softly that I must lean my ear next to her lips to capture what she says:

"Dale, you and your brother are so fortunate. Continue to be loving and kind and good to those whom God has entrusted to you," my eighty-nine-year-old aunt says, between labored breaths but with the ghost of a caring smile. "When you're at the end of your life, like I am, family is all that matters. If you've honored those you love, you'll be at peace. If not, you'll be filled with regret, and it'll be too late to do anything about it."

Two weeks later, she died.

When we are seriously ill, it's comforting to have friends visit or call and consoling to receive flowers or cards. But almost nothing can take the place of the support and love and caring and concern of family members. Under such circumstances, how healing and reassuring it is for both the patient and the loved ones to hear the words, "I care." Simply being there with love is often the gift that makes pain tolerable or a long night more peaceful.

The poet Robert Frost once wrote, "Home is the place where, when you have to go there, / They have to let you in." Most of us feel the truth of that statement. Most of those whose relationship with family have been strained sense on a very deep level that, tensions notwithstanding, family can be counted on in desperate hours. Sometimes, in fact, it takes a crisis to appreciate the value of what we have.

And those who are called upon feel the compelling bond, too. What parent would ignore even an adult child's call for help? What child would turn his or her back on a parent in need? Yes, some might, based on old hurts or current preoccupations. But in most cases the impulse to protect and assist a family member overpowers petty resentments. The force of family love gives us one of life's greatest gifts: the opportunity to step up and support one who has stumbled.

Certainly this was the case for my sister-in-law, Betty, who answered the telephone one warm Indiana morning in August 1995 to hear her brother's voice.

For Betty it had been a busy week, filled with many little activities, none of them terribly important. The last thing she expected was to hear from David. He had never really been a part of her life, and they had no common interests. After their parents' divorce (when she was nine, David sixteen), he moved out to live with his father, and all his adult life, he had remained distant. Although he was always invited to family gatherings, he rarely came. After their father died, David's remoteness continued. The last time he called Betty had been fifteen years ago when she moved from Florida to Indiana.

But as surprising as was his call, it was his message that surprised her even more: "Betty, I have been diagnosed with lymphoma."

A feeling of unreality swept over her as she listened. All of a sudden her stable, routine, quite predictable life had been turned upside down. While a doctor was monitoring David's progress and her brother had a network of friends he could rely upon, Betty reeled from the announcement.

After she hung up, Betty went immediately to the bookstore to learn more about the disease. She knew it was cancer, but the text identified three kinds: Hodgkins, non-Hodgkins, and AIDS-related. Betty became concerned that there might be even larger health issues involved.

"I need to know which one you have," she said to David the next day over the telephone.

"Non-Hodgkins," he replied.

Then on a Sunday morning one month later, just before she was to leave for church, the telephone rang. It was David again, and he said he was undergoing chemotherapy, and that the cancer was in remission.

"Wonderful," said Betty.

Then David added matter-of-factly: "Oh, by the way, I'm HIV positive."

It's hard to convey the disbelief that she felt. Like lightning the words shot through her, leaving her numb, speechless with panic. When a member of the family is suffering, no matter what the cause or how estranged he or she may have been in the past, all family members are affected. At such times each individual needs to keep a proper perspective on life and the importance of relationships. Despite the shock of David's revelation, helping him now became the family's number one goal, with little time left for judgment or recrimination. David's family rallied.

Betty called her two sisters. Her stepfather had known of the diagnosis for awhile, but their mother did not. Apparently David was relying on the family network to spread the word.

"Should I tell Mom?" Betty asked her stepfather, later.

"No," he said. "That's David's job. Let him do it his way." And he did, when he was admitted the following month to the hospital.

Although not obvious at the time, in reaching out to his family, David was giving a gift — an opportunity to reconnect, to reconcile. The way in which we die affects many people. "If I die with much anger and bitterness," says Henri J. M. Nouwen, "I will leave my family and friends behind in confusion, grief, shame, or weakness."

Desperate for prayers and somebody to talk with who understood, Betty shared her concerns at church. Desirée, a woman whose daughter, son-in-law, and nine-year-old granddaughter had died of AIDS, learned of her story, contacted Betty, and said, "You must come with me." That evening she took her to a meeting of Friends and Families of AIDS Patients.

It was this support group that helped Betty to understand what her brother would be experiencing, what he might be feeling. The participants gave her the encouragement she was seeking. And they described what she would face when she first went to visit David. One said, "God will guide you."

But nothing could quite prepare her for that first visit in October when she entered his hospital room: Curled up on the bed under a single sheet lay the five-foot ten-inch profile of what seemed to be a ninety-year-old man, frail and thin, ragged and emaciated, devoid of energy. He had lost all of his hair from the chemotherapy treatment for his lymphoma; his skin was gray. Already the effects of wasting syndrome — in which food passes through the body so quickly it has virtually no nutritious effect — were in evidence.

Dementia had also set in, caused by the AIDS virus destroying various areas of his brain. An MRI had revealed eleven shadows — or dead areas — and with time this condition would only worsen.

"Occasionally the brain kind of rewired itself," said Betty, "rendering him a few lucid moments when it sounded like he knew what he was saying and understood me, but those times were rare." It was obvious by then that David needed extra care.

On Thanksgiving Sunday, the news came from the doctor that he had found a hospice for David in Atlanta. It was this weekend, too, that all of his family came to be with David, even a sister from Alaska.

Haven House wasn't elegant, but all the nurses there were very, very loving and warm. They weren't afraid of touching the patients or of performing the most trying tasks with complete tact and selflessness. One six-foot five-inch male nurse carried the patients from place to place if they weren't able to be wheeled. The attendants caressed the patients, fed them, bathed them.

Every three weeks, Betty flew the five hundred miles from Indianapolis to be with David, four days each time. But visiting was also awkward because he did not want to discuss the fact that he was dying. "He believed he was going to go home soon," she said. "For a long time this closed the door to any heart-to-heart discussion."

Betty found some comfort in David's friend Clara, who had lost her own son a couple of years earlier to AIDS and had helped a co-worker to meet a peaceful death after his family had abandoned him. Now, like a protecting angel, Clara was there for David. She and her husband, Bill, had taken him to his doctor's appointments when he first fell ill. She knew what to do when he hallucinated. She knew all the medications and how they affected him. She was well versed in the handling of insurance.

"We couldn't have made it through without Clara," adds Betty. "Both she and her husband, Bill, were so ill themselves with a host of chronic ailments. But in spite of all their illnesses, they cared for David like he was their own son."

Betty is not sure what led to it, but during her fifth visit (there were seven in all), a window finally opened briefly, and she got to say what she really wanted to say.

"David, we've all known you were gay since high school. But it never mattered, any of it. Nobody ever said anything — it was a family secret nonsecret, like don't ask, don't tell. But I don't know if you ever realized that."

Then Betty added the all-important words: "I love you and I'll support you in whatever you need. Nothing's going to change that."

Some of the most poignant and unnecessary suffering experienced by the dying and their loved ones arises from the failure to connect with each other before the moment of death. Betty feels that she and her brother finally made that connection, to the benefit of both of them. "I wanted to do something to help David. I could not sit idly by. I desperately wanted him to know he was not alone, and my visits were almost as much for me as they were for him." On those trips, Betty had truly joined with her brother and with her family. A dying man came alive — and reached out with love to a world he had for so long kept at a distance.

Under such circumstances how can we truly connect with others? By showing the bedridden our understanding and friendship. By praying together. By reading Scripture together. By communing together in silence. By remaining open to God's leading. He will tell us what needs to be done, what should be said. What we receive then can be more satisfying to the Spirit than any amount of money, prestige, or power.

Two weeks after Betty's last visit to Atlanta, her mother called to say that David had died — one week shy of his forty-ninth birthday.

At the funeral, Betty and her family shared the same raw, deep agony. "When we grieve with family, strength is not necessary," she said. "We don't have to act any particular way, because they are grieving, too. We don't have to worry about our gestures, words, the expression in our eyes. With family we can't say or do anything wrong. We can completely let go."

Afterward, Betty expected her feelings would improve. She wouldn't have to watch David suffer so awfully, and she could dwell on the great gift that their reconciliation had given them both. But she couldn't have been more wrong.

"Now there was nothing I could do," she explained. "There was no action to be taken, nothing to fix. I had to accept that I was helpless to stop some things from happening, and to be willing to accept that God was in control."

But this was not an instantaneous act. It was seven or eight months before Betty lifted out of a deep depression and took an active interest in life again. She emerged from profound grief only with the passing of time and through the cleansing of prayer, her love for family and friends, and her belief in and submission to God.

"I now have peace in my acceptance of God's sovereignty. I thought I had it before, and maybe He's not done with me yet."

Perhaps not, for there is more to Betty's — and to David's — story.

"Everyone in life," said Bishop Fulton J. Sheen, "has at least one great moment to return to God." A month after his admittance to the hospice, David had joined the Presbyterian Church around the corner. A young parishioner who saw David's name and address listed in the Welcome New Members column of the church bulletin became his spiritual confidant. With Wayne, David discussed his impending death and spiritual struggles, awakening a heart long closed to much of the world. It was also with Wayne that David prayed and accepted Christ into his heart four weeks before he died.

There is great irony here. A month before his death, a man responds to God's gentle but persistent pressure and is reborn — his spirit, his soul, comes to life. He was moved by the love he received. He knew someone cared for him. Because of this, he believed that God must be even kinder and more generous than he had ever imagined possible. In effect, David came to understand that he was also a member of the family of God, and began to trust that the same love and acceptance he was receiving from his earthly family would also flow from his heavenly Father.

"After that, he never worried that he might be dying without God," Wayne said, later, "or that his disease might in some way be a punishment from God for something he did."

Rather, what David discovered is that no matter how many poor decisions he had made in his life, God hadn't given up on him. He felt God's presence in the room. He knew heart deep that God loved him even if he found it hard to love himself. The gift of love, freely given, sustained him to the end. When we are alive, there is always room for hope. "God's mercy," said Sheen, "is greater than [our] faults."

As Betty learned from talking with David's friends, however, many AIDS patients do not find the same love and support that he did. At such times the reaction of a family can be so very negative that it can shut that member off forever. It's especially ironic and tragic that the ill person's need for help and support can trigger the loss of it. And so some patients opt for silence.

"Because David did not know what my reaction would be," said Betty, "for a long while he chose to say nothing. David didn't know us very well. He had distanced himself so thoroughly. He was really worried that I would be condemning because I was a Christian. I was the one he worried about the most."

Back home, Betty saw some evidence of the kind of reactions David feared. From the start she was always open about what happened to him, and while some people were supportive, many were silent, while still others showed themselves indifferent, insensitive, or even cruel. One individual said, "Well, it's his own fault."

One of the most effective ways of counteracting the anger or judgment of another is to immediately say a prayer for that person. "By referring our enemies to God and by spiritually wishing them well," said Sheen, "we crush our own impulse to get even." Otherwise, we risk slipping into pride, and if in pride we look down on people, we can never look up to God. Great spiritual profit comes from loving those who hate us. As Jesus said, "Do not judge, so that you may not be judged" (Matt. 7:1).

We can also open ourselves up to others who are suffering. When Betty mentioned to the counseling pastor that she was eager to talk with anybody whose loved one has AIDS, he said: "Well, not many people are willing to admit that." She kept the offer open nonetheless.

"It has been four years since," said Betty, "and not a peep. But I am still available, and the counselor knows that."

Thomas Merton once wrote, "It is a foolish life which is lived in the minds of other human beings." Freedom is a gift. If we fear the judgment of others, we are slaves. Here I am reminded of poet Carl Sandburg's advice to his sister: "Live as your soul tells you how you ought to live. Listen to what others have to say, good and bad, about what you ought to do, and then do as your own soul, your own heart, your own self tells you." And so Betty continues to live out her faith. All that matters is that we seek to live in accord with God's will, ever mindful of His judgment lest we fall out of that will.

A greater awareness of how easily life can be taken also makes us sponges for the small moments. We start to enjoy our time with family, even when there is conflict. The conflicts subside much more quickly when we create the opportunity to reevaluate what's really important. Remembering how brief earthly life is encourages us to persevere and make the most of our time while here — even in a period of trial.

Years ago, a friend told Betty about her last months with her own mother, who was dying of cancer. Her mother, who was well off and well educated, told her daughter, "When it's all said and done, nothing matters but the people in your life."

"I have never forgotten that," said Betty, and reevaluating our priorities is something we should all do without being forced into it by a crisis like David's. Contemporary families expend so much time and energy on the quest for material goods and comforts that they fail to see the rewards that simple gifts of love can give. A relative doesn't need to be dying before we can step in with a helping hand.

Betty's experience with David showed her how to give and receive love, and helped her redefine what's important in her own life, reaffirm the universality of human suffering, and rededicate herself to alleviating it in whatever small way she can.

"I have also tried to become aware of the signals so that I might offer some relief, however briefly," she said. "If I can help someone find joy in life, even for just a moment, then it is a payment of gratitude to God for His grace. For in all our pain, there is joy to be had in the gift of life from God."

And our humble gifts of love to our fellow beings are treasures to our heavenly Father. Betty recalls as a child making a gift for her father. She took an eight-inch piece of scrap two-by-two wood, unsanded and bare, and tapped big common nails in the four corners of one length to make long legs; one nail on top made an upright tail; two small nails on the sides (bent down) formed ears; and the face on the end was made with roofing tacks hammered all the way in. Then she presented her creation to her father.

"What is it, sweetheart?"

"Um, it's a ring holder dog!"

That crude work of "art," says Betty, stayed on her father's dresser, holding his class ring on the tail at bedtime, for the rest of his life.

"Perhaps my father did not see the splintery ends," she said, "or the hammer blows that missed the nails and dented the wood, or the skill that was lacking. But he did see the love behind the effort, and it was enough. I saw all the flaws; but more than that, I saw his love in his acceptance of my lowly gift."

What gift can we possibly offer to our Creator who gives us life? None is sufficient, and yet anything given in love will be accepted in love and returned a thousandfold. Our skills do not matter, for it is the act of giving that counts. Our heavenly Father accepts the smallest effort on His behalf.

Betty's continued prayer is that the Lord will accept her gift of love through her actions every day. "Let all who see me or hear me know Your grace in my presence," she prays, "for it is your unwavering love that gives me strength." May that be our own prayer as well.

Indeed, one of God's greatest gifts to us is the opportunity to reach out, in love, for His sake. Sometimes He sends us into the lives of others to reassure them that He cares and has not abandoned them. What may seem at the time to be a chance encounter might very well be God's prevenient will at work.

Recently a friend of mine was on a flight home from Buffalo, New York. An older couple slipped into the seats next to her, holding hands. My friend commented on the lovely roses the lady was holding, but there was no reply.

"I figured something was amiss," she told me, "so I placed onto the lady's lap a miniature glazed angel pin that I had made. The lady gazed at me and said, 'How did you know?'"

"I didn't know anything," she replied, "but just thought you could use it." And then, without quite understanding why, she said to the lady, "You can endure through your faith."

They talked for the duration of the flight. The lady explained that they were on their way home to Seattle from attending the funeral of their daughter, who died at forty-one, leaving behind a husband and eight children.

When they landed and disembarked, the lady hugged my friend and said she would remember this trip forever. The gift had been so small but the effect was so great.

Of course, all families have joys and sorrows, trials and triumphs. But if ever there is a sterling example of the effect of parental love upon one's children in difficult times, it is evident in the family stories of Peggy and Bill Harding. Through their love and commitment, they have always encouraged their four children (and now eighteen grandchildren) to live moral, responsible, and generous lives.

With their son, John, who grew up in the 1960s, their relationship was not easy by any means. It was a tumultuous and confusing period, and in many ways he was a typical teenager, trying to find his identity or purpose in life.

"What amazes me now," he revealed, "is that in spite of serious doubts about my decisions, my parents always supported me and encouraged me to do and be my best. Even though they must have been totally disappointed in some of my decisions, I always knew they loved me." Never once does he remember them criticizing him or trying to make him feel that he had failed.

Many times, as he experienced the joys and difficulties of raising teenagers of his own, John prayed, "Lord, what should I do? How shall I handle this? What should I say? How should I act?" And so many times he has received the answer, "Well, what did your dad or mom do or say when you made the same mistakes?" The result is happy, productive children of whom he is extremely proud.

John appreciates his parents today because he has learned so much from their example. Were they perfect? No, of course not. Did they make mistakes? Yes, they did. But sometimes learning what not to do is just as valuable as learning what to do. And John has learned from their failures as well as from his own.

"They were proud of me when they had every right to be embarrassed by some of the things I did. They were patient with me when they had every right to be infuriated. They were loyal when they had every right to disown me. They encouraged me in the right ways even when they were disappointed in my decisions. They supported me when they didn't understand what I was doing. They forgave me when some of the things I said and did were unforgivable. But most importantly, they loved me when I didn't deserve to be loved. That, I think, is the most important lesson I have learned from my parents, that people need loving the most when they deserve it the least." He only hopes he has done and will continue to do as good a job as a parent with his children as they have with theirs.

Nancy Lynn, John's elder sister, feels similarly blessed. When her parents were married in 1947, and said, "For better or worse," they meant it. Many families have trials where one or both spouses could just "throw in the towel," or have children they could decide "just to write off." But Nancy's parents did not do that. Because of their commitment to each other and the love God gives them for each other, they have always stayed together as a family. "We have prayed together through the tough situations and seen God perform miracles in our hearts," she said.

What is her parents' legacy? Four children all married to their original spouses for a period of time from twenty-one to twenty-nine years. Eighteen grandchildren. One grandson-in-law with many more to come. "A family that is determined to love each other," said Nancy, "is committed to each other, and is serving God in four different states."

"If you want a happy family, if you want a holy family," said Mother Teresa, "give your hearts to love." What kind of love? In chapter 13 of his first letter to the Corinthians, Paul tells us: It is a love that "builds up," that is long-suffering, free of envy and egotism, that does not seek personal gain and is not easily provoked and thinks no evil thoughts of the other. How is that possible? Again, the Scriptures tell us: First, we must love the Lord our God with all our heart, and with all our soul, and with all our mind; and then our neighbor as ourselves.

"We are called upon not to be successful," added Mother Teresa, "but to be faithful." By establishing a strong relationship with God, we initiate and nurture relationships with other people through difficult times in an often perilous world. To participate fully in the human family, we must open ourselves to the spiritual and, in so doing, to each other. In learning to receive God's gift of love, we learn to give it to others.

family unity

Look to the living, love them, and hold on.

— DOUGLAS DUNN

$\mathcal{A}$s the story of Betty and the lessons she learned through David's illness illustrated, the test of familial love during hardship can be difficult but, ultimately, rewarding. It is for moments such as these, writes Harvard Chaplain Peter Gomes, that religion was made. "Contrary to the popular misconception, religion is not an escape from reality but rather a genuine effort to make sense of what passes for reality and all that surrounds it." When we rally around our loved ones, we help heal their wounds and at the same time strengthen our bonds with each other and with God.

Certainly there is no circumstance when the family is more important as a source of mutual support than in the time of a sudden tragic loss. What sustains the bereaved is the sheltering closeness of family, the indescribable bond that can cement together parents, siblings, and relatives, no matter how devastating the blow. In that communion of sorrow, families often find an indestructible core they never dreamed existed until tragedy revealed it.

Vivid in our national memory are the heart-stabbing images of families clustered together to endure the aftermath of the space shuttle Challenger explosion, of the Oklahoma City bombing, of school shootings, of tornadoes, hurricanes, and floods. At such times, most of us just want to drop whatever we are doing, rush home, and hug our loved ones. We are reminded once again of the fragility of life and of our own vulnerability. No one has promised any of us even one more day of living, and when a loved one is taken abruptly away, the family remains to close and heal the wound.

For the Jack Browne family, July 1998 was a golden time. His career as a lawyer was flourishing, and as an amateur magician he had the honor and privilege of serving the fifteen thousand members of the International Brotherhood of Magicians as their 1998–1999 International President. Wanting the companionship and support of his family to share the occasion of his inauguration, he invited twenty-nine members to join him in California for a reunion. It was a once in a lifetime effort that required time and money to get everyone there — but a small sacrifice that they have never regretted.

The photograph I have from that happy occasion shows his mother and father, the latter remarkably robust at age eighty-three and still practicing law in Marion, Indiana; his sister Jane Browne Bove and her husband, Tom, who flew in from their home in Miraval, southern France, and their five children; Jack's brother Tom, a physician in Evansville, Indiana, his wife, Lynda, and their three children; his sister-in-law, Lupe Browne, from Carmel, Indiana (his brother Jim, a very gifted lawyer and wonderful person, died a long slow death several years ago at the hands of leukemia), and their three children; and Jack's wife, Jan, and their five children.

"If you are counting," Jack said to me, "That's sixteen grandchildren, and my parents remembered every one of their birthdays."

Two months after the photo Jan and Jack were anticipating another family gathering, this one at Miraval. It would be a large party, but the site certainly would accommodate many guests. The restored château includes a vineyard, a freestanding chapel, an exclusive recording studio with swimming pool, a sizeable lake, a place for livestock, living quarters for workers, guest houses, and many other features that make up for the isolation of the compound and for the inconvenience of having to travel thirty minutes to a small village to furnish provisions.

Jane loved her role as hostess and always invited people who were going to travel in Europe to stop by. "She wouldn't wait for permission to enjoy anything," said her twenty-seven-year-old niece, Jenny. "She would find a way to make everyone — gardeners, nieces, millionaires, and salesgirls — feel like they knew something special about the world. She and Tom turned Miraval into the essence of life on some level, a place where people could get together, a great place to throw a party."

But the planned celebration never occurred. After dropping off her youngest daughter for college in Annapolis, Maryland, then visiting her parents in Marion, Indiana, Jane visited Tom's father in New York for his eighty-second birthday. Then she boarded Swissair Flight 111 to Geneva on September 2, 1998; normally, she'd have taken an Air France flight to Paris and Nice, but changed her routine because she wanted to visit her oldest son in Geneva. The plane crashed off Nova Scotia, killing all 229 people aboard.

"In these things you are always hopeful," said Tom of

his initial reaction to the news that evening. "You hope she missed the flight, you hope anything."

"You know in your heart she is dead," another family member said, "but it's too painful. You can't let go of hope right away."

At midnight, the confirmation came. Immediately, the Browne family networked by telephone. They all knew what they had to do without any discussion: Cancel whatever plans they had and fly to Indiana to be with their parents and with each other.

"On such occasions, no one can know what the survivors are feeling except the family," one family member said. "Others try to help, but they say things like, 'At least you had her for fifty years,' or 'She's better off in Heaven.' Without realizing it, they are trying to short-circuit our grief. Family members don't say things like that. They just cry together."

So the same Browne clan that had gathered in celebration two months earlier in Beverly Hills now gathered in grief in Indiana. This time they were twenty-nine in number, not thirty.

"Jane was always so cheerful," said Jack. "She immediately lit up any room she walked into. She made people laugh, sing, and dance." And so, that's what they did for three days in honor of her memory, knowing that that's what she would have wanted them to do. Although the tragedy was devastating to them all, their faith in God and the loving arms of family helped them through the three days they spent together.

Then something unpredictable happened. Even though he knew that no two people grieve alike and each person must cope with the intensity of pain in his or her own way, Jack thought for sure that Tom Bove and his children would cancel a planned trip to China. But as Jack said, "They decided to forge on without Jane, saying that they needed to make this trip she had so looked forward to, and to be together." And afterward, they still wanted the family to gather at Miraval, although it would not be the party they had planned.

The Brownes did have a modest celebration at Jane's favorite restaurant in Bourges, a small town in Provence an hour away. When they returned to the château, Jack was able to spend a long time meditating at the altar of an old stone chapel. He writes:

"Although raised a Methodist in Indiana, my spiritual quest began when I was a junior at the University of Wisconsin in 1959, when I became interested in the subconscious mind and, later, learned about meditation techniques designed to quiet the conscious mind so as to listen to the still, small voice within."

Through his lifetime experience, Jack said he has found certain places that favor meditation and provide deep peace, expansion of consciousness, and spiritual guidance. Among these places for him are Sedona, Arizona; Grace

Cathedral in San Francisco; and forests in Incline Village, Nevada, and Lassen County, California.

"But no place I have ever been has sent such strong spiritual vibrations coursing through my body and raising my consciousness as in the chapel at Miraval in September of 1998. There was something about the high energy of that spot and the comfort it gave me while grieving over my sister's death that made it very special indeed." Drawn to his own special place by the magnet of his family, Jack began to find solace and make peace with the loss of his sister.

After returning from Europe, Jack and Jan were making further travel plans from their home when the telephone rang. It was his father telling him in a calm voice, "We lost your mother last night. She died peacefully in her sleep."

"I knew my mother was in her eighties and that our physical bodies can carry on only so long," Jack reflected, "but I also knew how she had grieved over the loss of Jane, her only daughter. I am convinced that she had some more time left but instead died of a broken heart."

Only two months after Jane's death, the Browne clan converged on Marion, Indiana, this time twenty-eight in number, not twenty-nine. Again, they all knew at the time without discussion that they needed to be united to draw their strength from their bonds as a family and their mutual faith in God. They spent several peaceful days together and had a funeral service. They were concerned at the time about Jack's father, who was still heartbroken over Jane's loss in September. But he assured them he was all right and was planning to go down to Naples, Florida, in January, for a monthlong stay.

In mid-January, however, he checked into an Indianapolis hospital for elective heart bypass surgery.

"I spoke to him and my brother Tom the night before surgery," said Jack. "He was cheerful and told me that all would be well. That was the last time I talked with him."

Although the surgery was a "success," internal bleeding necessitated two more surgeries before the problem could be solved. The physical strain on the eighty-three-year-old was too much; he never regained consciousness. He fought valiantly for about two weeks, but died on February 2, 1999.

And so, for the third time in just five months, the Browne clan converged upon Marion again to grieve over the death of a family member. This time they were twenty-seven; although their numbers dwindled, their strength did not. In fact, they found a powerful reminder that there would always be others there for them to extend the hand of love and support. It's what families do.

Since then, the Browne clan keeps in close touch. Recognizing the important unifying powers of ritual, Jack's nephews and nieces work to sustain enduring family traditions and at the same time have initiated new ones. Instead of exchanging Christmas gifts, for example, each of them is assigned a family member to write a personal Christmas remembrance to. And every one of them has been provided with an attractive booklet showing the others' birthdays, since the matriarch and patriarch are no longer around to remember them.

Recently I looked again at the photograph taken of the Browne family reunion that July day in California. Three of the thirty smiling subjects — who coincidentally were all sitting together front-row center — would be gone within seven months. Yet this family has not only survived its tragedies, but become stronger because of them.

Jack says his parents' spirits abide with him always, as do the spirits of his late brother Jim and his late sister Jane. "I think of their departed souls often," he said. "When I do, I seem to hear them talking to me, giving me strength to help solve my problems."

Indeed, a strong family-oriented center can get people through the worst of times. When families have established the unity, caring, and mutual respect that comes from thoughtful, loving everyday interactions, they will be able not just to endure the stresses of extraordinary loss, but also to grow from them. They may find an even deeper level of familial devotion than they had ever dreamed possible.

When I think of the ideal of family unity, I recall also the Baker family, for several years our next-door neighbor in Indiana. Through their example I learned a lot about the universality of family difficulties and the power of love and devotion to overcome them. The parents' goal was to have thirteen children — a Baker's dozen. I always knew when a new baby was on its way, and not only because of the physical changes in the mother. Each morning I could hear the sounds of hammers and saws as an addition was built, or an extra wall created to divide a room in two. From a modest sixteen-hundred-square-foot home with three bedrooms, the Baker house slowly grew to occupy the entire backyard. When we moved away in 1969, they had nine children with another on its way.

What impressed me about the family was their secure, placid home, which served as the center of the children's religious and moral education. The family gave its members strength to overcome life's obstacles and taught them the value of selflessness. Mrs. Baker exemplified the courage and perseverance necessary to hold the family together. Her deep faith and clarity of purpose gave her family (and many of the neighbors) powerful lessons in the ways of loving, serving, and respecting our fellow human beings.

Secure in the affections of her parents, one of the daughters described her greatest desire: "to stay home safe with Mom and Dad, and help take care of the family. I only hope we may all keep healthy and be together."

In 1967, with Mr. Baker serving in Vietnam, the children and their mother remained at home, struggling to live as comfortably as possible under trying circumstances. As I later learned, financial collapse was a constant threat. One daughter developed pneumonia and almost died; another broke her leg. Mr. Baker was wounded in action and hospitalized. Understandably the days seemed dark, the house sad and lonely, as the family worked and waited while the shadow of death hovered over their once happy home. Through these potentially devastating trials, however, the family pulled together and grew even stronger. An onslaught of difficulties could not tear them apart.

But what happens, when, despite the family's best efforts and intentions, some trauma breaks down the sheltering walls and threatens its unity, safety, or well-being? On occasion children must be removed from their family when circumstances somehow shatter the family's stability. What can help those affected children to survive?

In World War II, for example, Anna Freud established nurseries in England for the care of hundreds of lonely, frightened, and confused children who had been sent away from their parents for safety's sake. For many of them, the nurseries turned out to be "psychological life-savers," wrote Robert Coles, "a place where affection and attentive understanding more than mitigated the strain and pain that accompanied the loss of the mother, especially, and the father."

In a very real sense, the supervisors became the children's parents as they tried to calm, reassure, encourage, and protect them until they could be returned to their homes; in essence, they created a surrogate "family," another safe place within which the children felt protected. The process remains in place in many conflicts even today, with various charitable organizations doing what they can to step in and rescue children from life- and soul-threatening situations. After such horrifying experiences, the children most capable of a return to normalcy are those who come from homes where they remember good family times together.

Detachment from the connections that compose the family unit can be devastating; yet the fact that many children not only survive this disruption but grow and thrive despite it speaks to the strength family unity can instill in its young members, even in a short time.

In her memoir *The Sacred Willow,* Duong Van Mai Elliott uses a wonderful expression for the resiliency of family in spite of upheavals, separation, and cultural ruination: "Like the willow, they have bent with the wind, but remain unbroken." This is a culture that still buries its dead in the corners of family rice fields, where parents until recently chose their children's spouses, where ancestral spirits are asked for guidance at household altars, where individuals consider parents and family before themselves, where the notion of "me" disappears into "we." As a Vietnamese proverb describes it, "Birds have nests; we have ancestors."

With much compassion, Elliott honors four generations of one family from the Duong clan in Vietnam. Born in 1941 to middle-class, French-educated parents, Elliott lived during the tumultuous years of the Japanese occupation, the Communist guerrilla incursion, the French colonial withdrawal, the country's separation into socialist North and capitalist South, and the arrival of American military forces and, with them, a new popular culture.

The Vietnamese say that no family will suffer ruin for more than three generations, that its fortunes will inevitably turn. Elliott tells how the Duong family rose to distinction six generations ago in a small village along the Red River, a place to which they had come to escape internal warfare. Two hundred years later, following several amazing reversals of prestige and wealth, we see the family dispersed again by civil war. Throughout it all, including sharp divisions of ideology, they remain a family loyal to itself and to each other.

Elliott's father, for example, became governor of the Haiphong area under the French and Emperor Bao Dai after World War II. Opposed to both the Communists and to French rule, Duong Thieu Chi barely escaped death at the hands of the French, Japanese, and Viet Minh forces. What sustained him through terrible hardships and imminent danger was his fierce desire to preserve his family. He and the author's mother, Nguyen Nhat An, had sixteen children, four of whom died in infancy; others grew up to become staunch supporters of the Viet Minh, while still others were persecuted and imprisoned for their anti-Communist sentiments.

Even in the face of political strife and outright warfare, Duong Thieu Chi, like his father and grandfather before him, remained unshakably loyal to his living family and his ancestors. A photo taken near the end of his life depicts the high value he placed on relationships: An aging Duong Thieu Chi, wasted by emphysema, stands aboard the USS *Hancock,* a refugee after the fall of Saigon — he is holding his little niece's arm.

Twenty years later and now married to an American, Elliott returned to her homeland and found that despite years of separation, two wars, and a revolution, her family had held together. Everywhere she was welcomed warmly by relatives. And by visiting the graves and standing on the soil that her ancestors once trod, she found a "sense of connection" to her forebears that the family stories and research had not created. "I had renewed family bonds unbroken by time and war," she wrote, "and I had reconnected with my roots and my native soil."

Whenever I am feeling too tired, too preoccupied, too restless, or too busy, I have only to think about the extraordinary courage and terrible ordeal of children of war, or the Vietnamese, or the Brownes, or so many like them. Instantly I emerge from any self-pity or dismay or selfishness or other egocentrism into which I had so easily slipped minutes before.

Indeed, most of our personal struggles dwindle in significance when set against the terrible trials that millions of families have had to endure. Oftentimes our problems are internal, of our own creation — a misspoken word here, a slight there, a silence. But during political or religious upheavals many families have faced an absolute life-or-death threat from a regime seeking to crush the human dignity of a minority group by attacking its center: the family. Such horrors put most contemporary Americans' problems in a proper perspective. What is clear is that such families blasted apart by political powder kegs almost universally sustain one goal — to be reunited in their homes once again. Family draws them back, no matter what.

That same spirit, I am convinced, is the core reason that the Hebrews have for five thousand years survived every kind of aggression and tribulation we can imagine. Most of the time during their history they lacked even a nation, but they survived as a people though they were scattered to the far corners of the earth. They endured and excelled. Why? They held onto the family — and to their faith in an all-knowing, all-powerful, all-loving God who, in His timing, would lead them through their difficulties and restore them to their families and to their homeland. They made it an indestructible foundation upon which to build — and sometimes rebuild — their lives. As long as the family or its influence endures, the individual, man or woman, adult or child, can find solid ground.

It doesn't require a huge imaginative leap to turn from the appalling reality of wartime to the dystopian vision of George Orwell's most famous novel, *1984*. What Orwell tells us so dramatically, I think, is that when human beings are disconnected from God, from any sense of community or family, from any reverence for the value of human life, they are capable of committing the worst of atrocities. His novel succeeds because it describes a complete *undermining* of the unity of the family and shows us the consequences.

Orwell envisioned a society whose citizens live a mindless life and are encouraged to lose themselves in such distractions as four-wall television, hearing-aid radios, high-speed travel, and group sports. Life is reduced to the norm of a mass audience. Education is devalued: School time is shortened, discipline relaxed, languages dropped, English and spelling gradually neglected and finally almost ignored completely. Life is immediate and one dimensional; only the job counts, and pleasure lies all about to fill the time after work hours. Why learn anything except pressing buttons, pulling switches, replacing the occasional nut and bolt? Imagine all this — and we have Orwell's picture of what Western society could become and does, in some aspects, already resemble. In *1984*, whatever is most valuable, humane, civilized, and decent has been reduced to the point of nonexistence.

There is a line of thought about the novel that looks at it optimistically: That Orwell set out to write the bleakest, most pessimistic, most nightmarish book he could in hopes that it would serve as a warning about what we may do to ourselves. The world of *1984* — with its drabness, loss of privacy, loss of love, corruption of art and language — is our world, deliberately exaggerated. Orwell wanted social change, but he also wanted a continuance of the eternal verities. When those are assaulted, our familial connections suffer.

While Orwell's cautionary tale is just that, a fiction, we know from experience that each family is, in its lifetime, assailed by stresses and events that are inevitably a part of the reality of human life. What helps us to abide these losses, traumas, and threats to our well-being, however, is the extraordinary variety of functions that families must perform. In spite of the ever changing sea of civilization, the God-given institution of the family has had a remarkably stable history.

the value of family

Family is the most important institution in America.
Just about everything of lasting value starts there.

— STEPHEN L. CARTER

Almost universally, we see ourselves as part of some kind of "family": sons or daughters, husbands or wives, parents or grandparents, sisters or brothers, even friends or neighbors.

What is a family? Considering how remarkably diverse and sophisticated the relationship can be, the question is more difficult to answer than we might at first suppose. Some even say the concept eludes definition. Certainly it is more than a household composed of parents and

171

children. More than a group of persons closely related by blood or marriage or adoption. More than a social construct. Will Durant called it "the nucleus of civilization." George Santayana called it "one of nature's masterpieces."

Perhaps many of us envision a family as a protective, close-knit circle of people, united in work and play, who unconditionally love one another, and live in peace without rancor or guilt. Or perhaps we envision a cold, impersonal household ruled by an exacting paterfamilias who inspires fear and trembling in its members.

Either scene is, however, a one-dimensional snapshot lacking depth and breadth. For as Scripture tells us and as history confirms, there is much more to the image. As the most important influence on our lives, the family is a divine institution, established by God to protect, promote, and perpetuate human existence. Cultures that have allowed their families to disintegrate, say many commentators, have quickly deteriorated or passed from the world scene.

"It is not good that the man should be alone," God says early in Genesis 2:18, thereby acknowledging, or perhaps establishing, that we are by nature social animals, unequipped to face the exigencies of life on our own. From the race's prehistoric days on, we have formed tribal bonds — "families" by blood or by choice — that allow us to fulfill our basic physical needs and satisfy our longing for companionship, stimulation, and meaning. All of us yearn to be nurtured, to be touched in the depth of our hearts.

For adults, family provides fulfillment; for children, family means survival. When infants enter the world, they are helpless, utterly dependent upon others, and unaware of where they came from, why they are here, or where they are going. Through the family's protection and discipline, its constant attention to material needs and to training, security, and guidance, children mature until they are able to provide for themselves and take responsibility for their own decisions and actions. The parents are also called to instill in their children norms and standards, to teach them how to evaluate situations in life, to train them when to say "yes" and when to say "no," to inculcate in them the principles of authority and self-discipline, and to model loving and generous relations to other people. "Train children in the right way," says Proverbs 22:6, "and when old, they will not stray."

While adults have many responsibilities within the family, children have only one: to respect their parents by listening to them, talking politely with them, obeying them. Love will follow as a natural consequence when the parents build a healthy connection and properly accomplish their job of training. A child is born willing and wanting to love his or her parents; the parents do not have to "earn" that love through permissiveness or overindulgence. In fact, the respect a child forms for parents who set reasonable boundaries only strengthens his or her love for them. We have all watched families in which one or both parents seem more concerned with their own need to feel loved than with their

child's need to learn about benevolent authority, consideration for others, and personal responsibility. A vicious cycle
of fear emerges, with parents desperately trying to please
children who hold less and less esteem for them.

In a family that is safe and nurturing, children can ask
questions without fear, experiment and take risks without
rejection, listen to their own inner selves, and develop an
independent spirit that encourages them to leave home
and travel on. After all, children are not our property but
gifts that we are to cherish, care for, and then give to the
community. If we keep reminding ourselves of this, then
when the time comes for them to set off toward their own
destination and join the larger "family" of the outside
world, says Henri J. M. Nouwen in *Reaching Out,* "we
might be more able to let them go in peace and with our
blessing."

One hundred years from now it will not matter what
kind of house we lived in, how large a car we drove, or
how much power over others we accrued. Neither will it
matter whether we provided our children with the most
expensive computer game or the trendiest clothes. What
will matter most is the effect we may have had on these
human beings that God has entrusted to us and to the
generations that follow. "The words that a parent speaks
to the children in the privacy of home are not heard by
the world," wrote novelist Jean Paul Richter, "but, as in
whispering galleries, they are clearly heard at the end, and
by posterity."

education

One day when our son turned seven and was lamenting all that was expected of him by his second-grade teacher, he asked me, "Daddy, how many years did you go to school?"

On a sheet of paper I listed "K" through "12," then "University 1, 2, 3, 4" and "Graduate School 1, 2, 3, 4, 5" and handed it to him. The next day I found the list taped to his bedroom wall. Next to "K," "1," and "2" he had printed a tiny red check mark.

The values introduced during childhood leave lasting marks, and certainly one of the most important values to instill in our children while at home is that of education. I fell under the influence of many great teachers whose examples attracted and inspired me, but I learned — *really learned* — from them because of my parents' passion for knowledge and their high expectations for my brother and me. Because of them, I believe, we grew to revere education.

In *The Soul's Code,* James Hillman reminds us that "a 'happy' child was never and nowhere the aim of parenting." An industrious, useful, malleable, healthy, obedient, mannerly, stay-out-of-trouble, God-fearing, entertaining child — yes. "But the parental fallacy has trapped the parents also in providing happiness, along with shoes, schoolbooks, and van-packed vacations."

As noble as these intentions may be, he continues, they

don't help a child find what he or she most needs in life: a sense of purpose. And a sense of purpose comes to us in part from a full and challenging use of the gifts we are given.

In my own family, as in millions of others, no gift was taken more seriously or exercised more strenuously than that of the human capacity for imagination and thought. "Your mind is a gift. Use it well." How often do I remember hearing those words! Or, "All we expect is for you to do your best."

Think of it, my father would say: The human brain is a grayish, three-pound gelatinous blob of chemical and electrical impulses occupying a few inches of space, that directs our thoughts, stores our memories, and triggers our fears. Locked within the human brain are anywhere from 10 billion to 100 billion nerve cells — neurons — nearly equal to the number of stars in the Milky Way. Each of these neurons may be connected to ten thousand other nerve cells, with some cells capable of receiving as many as one hundred thousand messages. At any given moment our brains may be processing an estimated 10 quadrillion to 100 quadrillion impulses, all in a fraction of a second. For an average eight-hour workday, the brain has a maximum capacity of something like 17 million memories. So to each of us God has given this gold mine between our ears all day, every day. We didn't earn it; we did nothing to deserve it. It's a gift, but a gift that, like a muscle, thrives on exercise.

And so, my brother and I knew that if we came home with average grades, or if we neglected our studies, then we weren't doing our best to use this miraculous gift. As if to reinforce this lesson, for years there hung in my father's study the idealized picture of a youthful Abraham Lincoln lying before a log fire and reading a book by its flickering light. It was a silent but very compelling reminder of a value important to our family, a message we couldn't ignore.

I suspect that the passion with which my father esteems education comes primarily from his own childhood experiences. Although he grew up in a loving, encouraging, and respectful home, his parents — while very intelligent — had neither the means nor the opportunity to pursue an education beyond high school, and so any drive toward that end had to come from within my father alone, or from others he met.

Tenacity, my father's determination to stay the course, may be his most uncommon quality. It marked everything he did, including his desire to learn and to emphasize the importance of learning to his sons. But it was not always so.

In 1939, when he was a junior in high school, education was of no interest or value to him. He attended school only because he was too young to leave, and coasted through his freshman and sophomore years with little effort, minimal studying, and even less motivation. Although he dreamed of going to college so that he could be on the football team, his lack of effort in the classroom made his goal seem highly improbable until the first day of his junior year.

That September morning was routine enough. He sat through several classes and then went to lunch in the gymnasium, where, after eating, he joined the rest of the "jitterbugs" on the gym floor as they danced to the music from the jukebox. Then he made his way to his fifth-period current history class. He slid into a seat, the bell rang, and the chattering stopped. Then it happened.

After placing his book on the desk, he looked up and noticed that the teacher was new: a tall, thin young man, black hair slicked black, wearing spectacles. For a fraction of a second, my father felt a vivid, almost palpable sensation: He was being given a second chance. This new teacher did not know the student he had been; this teacher would only know the student he was today — and tomorrow. The slate was wiped clean, and he was free to write on it anew. He could hardly contain his excitement. Inspired by hope, he was determined to make a fresh start. He had seen the person he could be.

From then on, he did excellent work, not only in history (for which he received his first A), but in all his subjects. After graduating from high school he went on to Massachusetts State College, where he played football for four years, was co-captain during his last year, and also did well academically as a zoology major. After the war, he earned his master's at Massachusetts and his doctoral degree at Pennsylvania State University; became assistant to the provost back at Massachusetts; served as director of a Purdue University–based committee representing a consortium of eleven major universities, which oversaw the development of cooperative graduate level programs; and finally, at the age of forty-nine, he became president of the University of Maine at Presque Isle where he remained for the next eleven years.

On paper, these steps might seem ready-made and easy to take, but in reality each represented a momentous, life-changing decision for my father. Robert Frost manages to convey just such a feeling in the final stanza of his poem, "The Road Not Taken":

> I shall be telling this with a sigh
> Somewhere ages and ages hence:
> Two roads diverged in a wood, and I —
> I took the one less traveled by,
> And that has made all the difference.

And the concluding sentence of philosopher William James's essay "The Will to Believe" — which my father had read and reread in class and carried with him throughout his academic career — suggests the difficulty of making such decisions and the positive attitude he had to adopt in order to survive: "If we take the wrong road we shall be dashed to pieces. We do not certainly know whether there is any right one. What must one do?...Act for the best, hope for the best, and take what comes." Certainly in his decisions about education, the right road was not necessarily the easy one. But every time he took the way he was most reluctant or felt the least prepared to take, he has been justified by the result. It created an example for my brother and me to follow not only in our own education but in other aspects of our lives as well.

Many years later, he told my mother more of the story of that signal day in his youth. The new teacher had been his main incentive to adopt a new attitude toward school, but he also felt moved toward change by a school friend and, oddly enough, by his dentist. His friend encouraged him and steadfastly assured him that he would go to college and also play football. That kind of assurance began to rub off. And when his dentist asked if he were planning on college and he replied that he was, the dentist asked, "Are you a good student? If you don't get good grades, you can't get into college." It made him realize that while other people believed in his ability to succeed, he had to work for that success; it wouldn't just happen without his own dedication to that goal.

God moves in mysterious ways, the old adage tells us, but sometimes the touch of His hand is almost tangible. The nudge toward change my father felt that memorable day in high school set his feet on the less-traveled but right path. And while he may not have realized it, telling my brother and me that story during our formative years focused our own eyes on the importance of education and provided for our souls a valuable example of how God can guide us toward positive change if we just let Him.

reading

Along with education, there is no place like home for learning the value of a lifetime devoted to reading. I had the good luck to be born into a family that has always loved to read, and although at Christmastime my brother and I were happy with such gifts as skis, clothing, and the like, we would have been greatly disappointed if there had been no books.

"Respect your mind and use it," my aunt would advise. "Don't ever stop. Make reading a way of life, and use what you learn in service to others. A family that reads together, grows together."

After an afternoon of conversation with her, I wanted to rush out and read everything I could get my hands on. My parents still have that effect on me.

My mother cannot recall the first time she held a book, but she does remember being read to as a child and how often her father told her stories about his boyhood.

"He always began with the words, 'When I lived up on the farm....'" she explained. "What happened there must have been exciting, because every night I asked for another story. It was a pleasing, comfortable refrain, and I enjoyed the stories as one enjoys a favorite song."

At an early age my mother was given a book called a "primer." The green cover was well worn, leading her to believe that other members of the family must have read it, also. What it contained, she can only guess. But in the

back of her mind she sees words beginning with each letter of the alphabet along with pictures describing the
words.

"I wish I had it now," she said. "What memories the
book might evoke; it is as much a reflection of my childhood as the teddy bear that was left behind when our
family moved."

My mother's fondness for books is not limited to the
fact that she loves to read. Books are a palpable presence
for her. The American bibliophile Alfred Edward Newton
once said, "We cherish books even if unread; their mere
presence exudes comfort, their ready access, reassurance."

One of the rooms in the house where my mother lived
as a child at one time had bookcases lining a wall, and she
says she remembers how pleasurable it was to sit there
alone, reading each title and author, exploring the names
as some children explore a forest or an attic brimming
with treasures: *Moby-Dick, A Tale of Two Cities, Silas
Marner, Kidnapped.*

"Although no words were spoken," she added, "I
sensed that we were friends. Somehow they had contrived
to make me aware of them, and I spent time getting to
know who they were."

For her, books have always had a certain texture and
distinctive odor that are vivid but ineffable. In *One Writer's
Beginnings,* novelist Eudora Welty confirms that she is
unable to "remember a time when I was not in love with
them — with the books themselves, cover and binding

and the paper they were printed on, with their smell and their weight and with their possessions in my arms, captured and carried off to myself."

My mother's father liked detective stories. She's not certain, but she always suspected that the books her mother enjoyed were those with a romantic flavor. And every night Aunt Katie, a former teacher, went into the front room and settled down with a book in her hands.

"I also remember my sister sitting by the window, reading, when we were children," my mother said. "Her total absorption fascinated me: From the moment she opened a book, nothing disturbed her. I seldom 'lost' myself in a book, but that did not interfere with my reading pleasure. Perhaps the ticking of the clock, the slamming of the screen door, the ringing of the telephone, and voices in the background were musical accompaniment to the scenes playing out in my imagination as I turned from page to page."

It should come as no surprise, therefore, that our family's passion for reading has been lifelong and powerful. Because my brother and I grew up inside a home filled with books, and because our parents and grandparents and aunt seemed always to be reading, we were encouraged to do the same. Our love for books grew as we did.

In the solitude of our bedrooms, or sunk into the cushion of the living room sofa, or in the backyard hammock on a lazy summer day, we had the privilege of reading uninterrupted to our hearts' content. Saturday morning was a favorite time because I could lie in bed until noon, reading. Or late at night, lights off, snuggled under the covers with a flashlight and my latest acquisition from Junior Scholastic Books.

For my eighth birthday my father built a bookcase. It ran the length of one of my bedroom walls, and I loved to arrange and re-arrange my books on its three shelves. Nancy Drew mysteries, Robert Louis Stevenson, C. S. Lewis, Agatha Christie, Sherlock Holmes, science fiction of any kind, horror tales — these were among the early books that fed my imagination.

Nothing could quite compare to the exhilarating journeys of the mind on which various authors took me: voyages to India, to Africa, to much of Europe, to most of America's states, to the Mayan ruins, the Egyptian pyramids, the Alps. I was entranced as I descended twenty thousand leagues under the sea, stared into the eyes of a *Tyrannosaurus rex* and a raptor, climbed to the peak of Mount Everest, rode into orbit aboard a spaceship, and left my footprints in the dust of Mars, Venus, and Mercury.

In other words, many delectable books took me out of my own life and into someone else's, and the sheer pleasure of that transposition was an attraction in and of itself. I have never been so unhappy that, along with nature and prayer, *reading* hasn't helped me.

When Gail Sheehy wrote her biography of Soviet president Mikhail S. Gorbachev, she discovered that all of the educated Soviet citizens whose homes she visited keep their books "enshrined in the central altar of the apartment — often glass-enclosed on lovingly handmade bookshelves and adorned with vases, dried flowers, even crucifixes — very much like the altars of the medieval monasteries that have survived in the countryside." Whenever they removed a book, and caressed it while they described the precious contents for a visitor, Sheehy was reminded of Pristavkin's metaphor: "Literature is the expression of [the] conscience and spirit of the people. Your friend can betray you, the woman you love can betray you, but a book — never."

My father discovered much the same to be true in the homes he visited during a ten-day trip to Poland in 1978.

What I didn't realize then but have come to see over the years, however, is the valuable role reading can play in enhancing our relations with others. By experiencing, even vicariously, another's pain or puzzlement or perspective, we broaden our insight into the human condition and deepen the level at which we think and feel. We learn what qualities and feelings and desires we share with others who in culture or generation or outlook may seem to be very far from us. In other words, we learn about not just what makes humans different, but also what makes them the same.

"You think your pain and your heartbreak are unprecedented in the history of the world, but then you read," said writer James Baldwin. "It was books that taught me that the things that tormented me the most were the very things that connected me with all the people who were alive, or who had ever been alive." And such knowledge, along with the nurturing, teaching, and modeling provided by our family of origin, is essential in developing our potential for relating to others. Through reading we can learn to be members, not just of our own families, but of the family of humankind.

"Do you read a book a week?" a student asked me one day in class, without trying to hide his sarcasm.

"No," I said, after a suitable pause. "I don't read a book a week. I read four or five books a week."

Usually, I would not have responded at all, but I felt that the other students deserved to hear the truth — because implicit in his question was an underestimation of the importance of books in my life as well as in the lives of many of his peers.

Until quite recently, it had not occurred to me that reading was in need of defense. I have always looked upon it as a wholesome and familiar part of life, natural and indispensable, calling for no explanation. Yet all too often I encounter students who cannot name the last book they read for pleasure; and I am always struck by how many otherwise handsomely appointed American homes have no books in sight.

The names "bookworm" or "nose in a book" still have a negative connotation — when spoken by the nonreader — implying readers are "lazy, aimless dreamers," and, says Anna Quindlen, "people who need to grow up and come outside to where real life is, who think themselves superior in their separateness."

In fact, the opposite may be true. Those who read are very much in touch with life, in some cases, too much so. In her memoir *I Know Why the Caged Bird Sings,* Maya Angelou speaks movingly about the important role that reading played in her early life.

When she was four, her parents divorced and sent Maya and her brother, Bailey, to live in the rear of a Stamps, Arkansas, store with their grandmother and uncle. No explanation was offered; no assurance was given. On many nights the two children huddled together, alone, and cried and wondered, "Why did they send us away?" "What did we do so wrong?" A year later, Maya fell in love with the plays of William Shakespeare. As she says, the line from Shakespeare's "Sonnet 29" — "When, in disgrace with Fortune and men's eyes" — was a state with which she felt herself "most familiar."

During the next few years, her sorrow was compounded by the indignities of racism, sexism, and, worst of all, at age eight the horror of being molested by her mother's boyfriend, Mr. Freeman. Her subsequent courtroom testimony led to his conviction and soon thereafter his mysterious death. So traumatized did Maya become that she withdrew into herself and, except for rare moments with her brother, Bailey, refused to speak. She simply adopted silence. She lived in a cage of her own creation.

But Mrs. Bertha Flowers, a kind and discerning neighbor, sensed her pain and helped Maya open the barred door. She first left a book with the sad child, knowing she would read it out of obligation, then, later, opened her own book collection to the girl. Maya spent the next year reading voraciously — nonfiction, poetry, fiction, drama — trying to come to terms with the pain and rejection that she felt, trying to find some answers. As she says, "To be allowed, no, invited, into the private lives of strangers, and to share their joys and fears, was a chance to exchange the Southern bitter wormwood for a cup of mead with Beowulf or a hot cup of tea and milk with Oliver Twist." She read, and she waited.

Finally, almost a year after Freeman's death, she began to speak, and did she have things to say! She emerged from her cage and began to sing — through her own poetry and essays. Reading had helped her to keep sane and to find herself; it had shaped and nourished her inner life as a child. Reading had helped her to emerge without bitterness, without anger. Like the protagonist in Roald Dahl's *Matilda,* "She had learned something comforting, that we are not alone."

Renowned violinist Isaac Stern once described an experience he had as a pupil of the great cellist, Pablo Casals.

Imagine yourself suddenly coming upon a [high brick] wall, not knowing that beyond it lay an exquisite garden. What Casals did was open a door into the garden; you entered and suddenly found yourself amid colors and scents you never dreamed existed. He revealed what might be accomplished once you were inside the garden. But how many of the colors and scents you could make your own, giving greater power to your musical imagination — that was your responsibility.

A child's family can be instrumental in opening that door, in showing the way to a rich and colorful and limitless reading life. Where reading is nurtured, insight, knowledge, and love will bloom. As our minds grow, we are able to help others grow. "A book is like a garden carried in the pocket" (Chinese proverb).

integrity

But of course education does not occur only in the classroom or with a book. What we think matters very little if we lack the courage of our convictions, the willingness to act and speak in behalf of what we know to be right. Along with the value of education and reading, the home is also a place for transmitting the value of integrity.

"The longest journey a person can take is the twelve inches from the head to the heart," an old proverb says. Who is helping our children to make this journey? In Western civilization the cornerstone for integrity is the Ten Commandments. In many homes, these laws are taught so early and so thoroughly that they sink to the bottom of the child's mind, where everything that comes along later settles on them.

Jack Miles has called the Ten Commandments the "least culture-bound moral code ever written." (See Exod. 20: 1–17.) Indeed. Every year legislators write and pass more and more state and federal laws, and more and more interpretations of those laws. The irony is that, with obvious exceptions, what a family needs to know to live a balanced, fruitful life is contained in ten simply worded, direct laws delivered with urgent insistence to the Hebrews over five thousand years ago.

The first four center on love and respect for God, on establishing and maintaining a proper reverence for the Almighty: (1) "You shall have no other Gods before me," (2) "You shall not make for yourself a graven image," (3) "You shall not take the name of the Lord your God in vain," (4) "Remember the sabbath day, to keep it holy."

Built upon the foundation of the first four, the remaining six concern relationships within the human family: (5) "Honor your father and your mother," (6) "You shall not [murder]," (7) "You shall not commit adultery," (8) "You shall not steal," (9) "You shall not bear false witness,"

(10) "You shall not covet." This sequence is significant: Unless we have established a meaningful relationship with God, meaningful relationships with other people are impossible. "Intimacy with God," said U.S. Senate Chaplain Dr. Lloyd John Ogilvie, "means integrity of life."

Here then is the bedrock of God's intention for us, our families, and our communities. Here we find the secrets to freedom from the self-destructive behaviors that can tear at the fabric of our lives and rob us of the joy, peace, and purpose that God has promised. No institution — including the church — can take the place of the family in teaching children to abide by these laws where they play and work and live. Children have to see this moral code in practice on an everyday basis, and that starts in the home.

In the summer of 1969, when I announced to some of my Indiana friends that I was moving to California to begin graduate school, one exclaimed:

"California! Why there? You'll be subjected to temptations you can only begin to imagine!"

While well-meaning, my friend's comment didn't show much faith in my character. But he did have a point: Away from home, away from all who knew me, I would be tested. Parents can give us good advice, they can put us on the right path, but the final focusing of our character lies in our own hands. Integrity is a decision. We don't just fall into it.

I will always remember my first semester as a professor at Citrus College. It was early November 1973, and I was teaching a section of English 101, a demanding course on our campus that requires the student to read and write a great deal.

This particular day I had collected the students' written assignments, and reading through them that evening it soon became obvious to me that one of my pupils had committed plagiarism. Well, all of us make mistakes, I thought, and I didn't want to spend the time and energy searching for the source of the material. So the next day in class, I said, *"One of you has copied your paper from an outside source. At the end of class if you will come to me and tell me why you did that, I will give you the chance to rewrite your essay. Otherwise, I am afraid that you will have to receive an F for the semester."*

At the end of class, *three* students came forward!

At least these students had the courage to come take responsibility for their actions. They learned a lesson in integrity.

Plato's answer to the question "Why should I be a person of integrity?" is "Because it is healthier for the soul." The word *integrity* comes from the same Latin root as *integer* or *integrate*. Historically, it has been understood to carry much the same sense, the sense of *wholeness* as Webster defines it: "a person of integrity, like a whole number, is a whole person, a person somehow undivided." It connotes completeness, serenity, living rightly, doing right. Integrity helps us understand what is right, and to do it, even when there is a cost.

In his brilliant book *Integrity,* Stephen L. Carter, professor of law at Yale University, identifies three steps that integrity requires: "(1) *discerning* what is right and what is wrong; (2) *acting* on what you have discerned, even at personal cost; and (3) *saying openly* that you are acting on your understanding of right from wrong." *Discerning,* he says, requires a degree of "moral reflectiveness." *Acting* denotes the ideal of a person of integrity as steadfast, as one who keeps commitments. *Saying* reminds us that "a person of integrity is unashamed of doing the right."

In the same book, Carter relates how his first lesson in integrity came the hard way. The year was 1960 and he was a first grader in Harlem. Carter and the other students were sitting in a circle. One by one each child would put on a blindfold and then try to identify by touch each object the teacher handed to them. Those who guessed correctly got to stay in for the next round; those who did not had to leave the circle. To the astonishment of his classmates, Carter survived almost the entire game, until the teacher discovered that he was peeking from beneath the blindfold. He writes:

"Fortunately for my own moral development, I was caught. And as a result of being caught, I suffered, in front of my classmates, a humiliating reminder of right and wrong: I had cheated at the game. Cheating was wrong. It was that simple."

The moral opprobrium that accompanied the shame he felt has stayed with him all these years — which, he adds, "is exactly how shame is supposed to work." As he grew older, whenever he felt tempted to cheat — at a game, on homework — he would recall his teacher's "stern face and the humiliation of sitting before my classmates, revealed to the world as a cheater."

(When I related this story to my twelve-year-old son, he said, "I couldn't even take the pressure of a lie. If I told you one, I would have to admit it within a day. That's just the way I am." What a blessing to hear those words!)

Like all good things, integrity builds on itself: Children who see their parents do what is right, even when there is cost, are most likely to do the same upon reaching adulthood. I have heard it said that true character is what we are when nobody's looking, in the secret chambers of the heart. Speak the truth, confess to God regularly, live consistently: God wants our children's hearts as well as their heads.

faith and prayer

Hardly anything can give a loved one greater assurance than when someone says, "Let's pray!" or "I will pray for you." Those few words, if delivered with tenderness and conviction, speak of the deepest level of human concern and connectedness. Parents need to know how to put prayer to work for themselves and their families. They need to develop in themselves a sense of coming earnestly and expectantly to God. Then they can teach their own children to do the same. Prayer, like all good habits, is best learned when we are young.

Sadly, however, the one place where spirituality *should* be freely cultivated — within the family — is all too often spiritually barren. Many parents have lost their faith and any kind of dependency on God.

Once when Rabbi David Wolpe spoke to a group of six hundred children in Dallas, Texas, he asked them, "What would your mother say if you asked her what she thought about God?" A girl in the front row jumped up and waved her hand. Her answer was brief and memorable: "She would say, 'Ask your father!'"

"How sad, how tragic," says Rabbi Wolpe, "that so many parents strive to do their best for their children, and take great pride in being open in discussing the most intimate issues with their children. But when our children broach the most important questions in life — Is there a God? Are we alone in the universe? Where do moral rules come from? — we are silent....Soon, our children learn not to ask."

Indeed, with respect to family life, the words *God* and *soul* have almost been eliminated from our family discussions, and when we try to exist without them we easily become victims of a mindless quest for happiness that is devoid of hope or comfort. We sleepwalk through life. Much contemporary art, literature, and music, for instance, bombards us daily with images of a world that seems out of control — "dense, opaque, and unintelligible," as one commentator put it — and we seem to be helpless facing it. "The richer we have become materially," wrote Martin Luther King, Jr., "the poorer we have become morally and spiritually." All around us we hear only cries of pain. Why? Is there something about ourselves that has become confused, lost, without an anchor?

Psychiatrist Carl Jung said that the great neurosis of our time is the neurosis of emptiness. In losing the fundamental connections the family gives us, we have cut ourselves off from the root of our being and from God, and by so doing we experience great emptiness and an accompanying loss of purpose, which lead to rootlessness, apathy, and a dead or dying self.

But we are not *human* beings on a spiritual journey, philosopher Pierre Teilhard de Chardin reminds us; we are *spiritual* beings on a human journey. As Thomas Moore wrote, many traditions imagine the soul as an "immense space, an innerscape as vast as the outerscape of the universe," deep within whose core there resides a desire to live as richly and as deeply as possible. Children by nature and by instinct want to enjoy life to its fullest, to satisfy their truest desires, to develop their own potentialities so as to achieve the best that is in them. They also want parents who treasure the days that are spent in their company. If we fail our children in these respects, they may well be condemned to a life deeply colored by frustration, confusion, anger, or perhaps worst of all, apathy.

A shared trust in God binds together a family; without it, we are morally adrift.

And so if we are at all wise and sensitive to our responsibilities and opportunities, we will encourage and nurture our children in the direction of their souls, and that begins with prayer.

What is prayer? It is a way to make contact with God, to feel His presence ever more surely. "I can take my telescope and look millions and millions of miles into space," said Sir Isaac Newton, "but I can lay it aside and go into my room, shut the door, get down on my knees in earnest prayer, and see more of heaven and get closer to God than I can assisted by all the telescopes and material agencies on earth."

The rabbis called prayer "the service of the heart." It has also been variously defined as the interior life; a way of loving others; an intimate, ongoing interaction with God; a request; or a petition. St. Augustine defined prayer as a turning of the mind and heart to God: "True, whole prayer," he wrote, "is nothing but love." Prayer, said St. John Vianney, "is the inner bath of love into which the soul plunges itself."

But perhaps the most apt description is what a child might give: the soul talking with God. If we want to have intimate fellowship with God, and if we want to know the whole will of God and to experience fully the transforming power of His presence in our lives — then we must talk to Him and we must listen. We must work as hard on our relationship with Him as we do on our relationship with our families. We must reveal ourselves and our doubts and fears, we must ask our questions, and affirm our faith. We must pray to explore our own souls and to realize the wonder of His love.

"O Love that wilt not let me go," wrote hymn lyricist George Matheson in 1882. The desire to feel love and guidance is a universal human trait; we want and need that hand to hold, those ears to hear, those arms to embrace us with their comfort and strength. If we are fortunate, our parents and other family members provide for most of those needs. Even more steadfast is God's comfort and strength; God is there for us, nurturing us physically, emotionally, and spiritually, and to truly feel that love and support, we must seek it through our words with Him.

And what a privilege it is to enter into the very presence of that love! We do so, says A. W. Tozer, "because, and only because, He has first put an urge within us that spurs us to the pursuit." If that is accurate, and I believe it is, then it was His "still, small voice," blended with my mother's, that urged me forward as a child in my own prayerful life.

I began by learning the Lord's Prayer from Matthew 6:9–15 (KJV), which I recited every night with my mother after I was tucked safely into bed with the lights off. In the dark I couldn't see her, but I could feel her reassuring presence and hear her soft, loving, confident tones as she began, "Our Father which art in Heaven...." Then she followed with a prayer that is a favorite of many children: "Jesus, tender shepherd, hear me, bless thy little lamb tonight. Through the darkness be thou near me. Keep me safe 'til morning light."

In time, I was able to commit these words to memory, and soon they became my constant companion in every conceivable setting. Later, she gently encouraged me to memorize some of the Psalms, starting with the Twenty-Third: "The Lord is my shepherd; I shall not want...." Those words, too, went deep into my mind and heart to become my own, informing and shaping my spontaneous expressions of prayer as I learned to voice my innermost concerns and desires with confidence and submission. "No matter what you're doing," my mother would say, "you can pray — anywhere, at anytime."

"Pray without ceasing," Paul admonishes us in 1 Thessalonians 5:17, and the Scriptures are unremitting in their insistence that, in moments of happiness, moments of pain, when seeking answers, when grateful, when merely expectant, we should pray. Speak without fear. Share your whole heart. Be honest. Cast all your cares upon Him. No matter is too small or too great to be of concern to God, but first we must bring it before His throne of grace. God intervenes in all areas of life. When we are grounded in prayer, even our activity becomes more efficient, more creative, and more energized. "Every one of us needs half an hour of prayer each day," wrote St. Francis de Sales, "except when we are busy — then we need an hour." The more often we pray to the Father, the more dependent upon Him we become.

Something special happens when families pray together. Jesus said, "Truly I tell you, whatever you bind on earth will be bound in heaven, and whatever you loose on earth will be loosed in heaven. Again, truly I tell you, if two of you agree on earth about anything you ask, it will be done for you by my Father in heaven. For where two or three are gathered in my name, I am there among them" (Matt. 18:18-20). Mother Teresa said in many interviews:

> The fruit of prayer is faith;
> the fruit of faith is a clean heart,
> and a clean heart can see God.
> The fruit of prayer is the deepening of faith;
> the fruit of faith is love,
> and the fruit of love is service.

That puts faith in perspective. That's the secret of a caring, complete life. God listens to and answers prayer.

When I think of a prayerfully led life of integrity and faith, I am reminded particularly of my paternal grandmother, Angeline. She stood five-feet-four: average height or a little over for one born at the end of the 1880s, rather short compared with her grandchildren's generation. Hers was a handsome face, with somewhat broad cheekbones, a mouth well shaped and strongly defined and — her most striking feature — eyes that looked intensely, as if welcoming life with eager curiosity and acceptance.

Her faith had been tested many times: her exodus by

ship in 1913 from Krakow, Poland, to America when she was only fifteen, never again to see her homeland or parents; the long hours she and her husband worked in the silk mills just to make ends meet while raising and supporting four sons; the near death at age five of her third son, my father, whom she prayed over without ceasing and nursed back to health after the doctors had given up hope and a priest had administered last rites; the long war years when she awaited the safe return of her four sons; the loss of her second son, Teddy, to cancer at age sixty-two; the death of her husband in 1979; and her own final illness. Yet, just before slipping away, she said to her gathered family with absolute certainty, "I see Jesus!"

To this day I cannot fathom how my grandparents (as mere children) survived when on a bright and bitterly cold December day in 1913 their respective parents took them to a ship, hung a sign with a strange name around their necks, said good-bye, and left them. Their parents had no choice, of course, but they did not understand that until much later.

On the one hand, my grandmother was tough, strong-willed, confident. On the other, she had a velvet touch. Her generosity toward others always exceeded her means. I remember my last visit to see my grandparents early in 1979. At one point when she and I were alone, she slipped — as she often had when I was a child — some folded currency into my hand.

"Don't tell grandpa," she whispered.

"I won't," I said, and then before I left I secretly slipped the forty dollars back into her purse.

She was a devout Catholic who saw God in everyone she met. How often in my mind's eye do I see that tiny bottle of holy water in the kitchen and always within easy reach in times of trouble, of illness. But I remember most of all a Polish Bible resting on a polished mahogany stand, under a crocheted cover on an end table in the living room. Other than a few articles of clothing, that Bible was the only item she was allowed to take with her when she was sent from her homeland. It was barely intact: pages as thin as tissue and so worn and soft they could be rolled like a magazine, with covers whose gold filigree lettering was so weathered it was only visible if the book were tilted sideways in the sunlight. But still my grandmother read and reread, and always with an eye to meeting God.

"Reading is fuel for the fire," Abbot Hugh Gilbert has said. "Prayer is the flame, but you won't have a fire if you don't have fuel." By feeding herself with the Word of God, my grandmother put fuel into the hearth of her heart, and there was prayer. My brother and I can still hear her voice, strong and full of love, as we left her home after each visit: "God bless you!"

I have no doubt that my father's reverence for God and his own reliance upon prayer relates directly to his mother's faith. By her example and encouragement, she effectively and powerfully planted the seeds of faith in the little spirits, the young minds of all her sons — and watched prayerfully as the seeds took root and eventually grew to fullness — to be passed on to their own children.

Prayer, like all good habits, is best learned while we are very young. With so much suffering in families these days all over the world, Mother Teresa believes that it is important not only to pray but also to forgive: "People ask me what advice I have for a married couple struggling in their relationship. I always answer, 'Pray and forgive'; and to young people who come from violent homes, 'Pray and forgive'; and to the single mother with no family support, 'Pray and forgive.'"

Prayer can and does work. It strengthens our relationship not only with our Maker, but with our fellow sojourners on this Earth. It forges powerful bonds of loyalty, self-sacrifice, and caring for members of our family and our community. Prayer may be the lifeline of the soul, connecting us with God as we endure stormy seas and calm, but also, as we learn in the following story, it is a beacon that can guide the direction of our familial craft toward a safe and peaceful harbor.

A ten-year-old boy was sent on an errand by his father. The night was dark, there was no moon, and the destination was a long way from home.

"I am afraid, Daddy," he said. "This lantern lights such a little bit of the way."

But the father was a wise man. He took the little fellow's hand in his, went as far as the garden gate, and then, releasing the boy, he said, "Now, son, you can see the light always goes ahead of you. It is not necessary to see all the way to the barn. All you need is light enough to take the next step."

And so like a lantern in the dark, prayer should be our first resource, not our last resort. "It's a powerful force, prayer is," Abbot Dom MacDonald said. "God help anyone, or anything, that tries to stand in its way."

The family that prays together does stay together. So it has always been, and so it always shall be.

solitude

At one time or another every family member, however, needs time apart. A call to solitude can come upon us at any moment, under any circumstances — during times of good health or the trials of infirmity, after abandonment by or the death of a loved one, in childhood or later in life, in crowds, voluntarily, or imposed. Sometimes, it sneaks up on us, much like the persistent ache of a hunger that, despite the human connections we've established, no sustenance from our fellow human beings can satisfy. Or it beckons as a still, quiet voice from within — the voice of God.

At such moments we may feel a desire, as essayist and poet Henry David Thoreau did well over a century ago, to retire from the presence of others, to go to the woods to "live deliberately, to front only the essential facts of life," to remove ourselves from peripheral concerns, from the pressures of a madly active world, and to return to the center where life is sacred — a humble miracle and mystery. Nothing could be worse, Thoreau wrote, than to come to the end of life and "discover that I had not lived."

As Thoreau suggests, in confronting "only the essential facts of life" we meet ourselves face-to-face, and that experience can be rewarding, often life changing, raising us to the heights of ecstasy, self-awareness, and creativity. In solitude, we may find a new beginning, an opportunity to break old habits. In solitude, we may find increased sensitivity, compassion, and empathy that we can take back to those we love. In solitude, we may find the truth of ourselves, restore our dulled senses, and clarify and reorder our priorities. In solitude, we can sort out what's important about those relationships that help to define us. Above all, in solitude, we may find God, and come to hear that voice.

Like so many proponents of thoughtful solitude, my own enthusiasm for it began in childhood. Although not necessarily a loner, even then I felt naturally inclined to spend long stretches of quiet time alone; I would take walks, read, or listen to music, or just lie down and venture, I suppose, as deeply as I could into myself. I came to trust the soft, internal voice that speaks so eloquently on every decision in life, that helps us to find out what is best for ourselves and our own nature.

Fortunately, my brother and I had parents who understood, supported, and even encouraged our inclinations; indeed, "quiet time apart" became as natural for us as perpetual noise and confusion seemed to be for our next-door neighbors. We treasured our time together as a family, but we also welcomed our time apart, and our intimacy with and understanding of one another grew richer as a result.

Unfortunately, in a secular world that devalues those who make time to listen to themselves, in a society that tends to equate a need for solitude with laziness, inactivity, and nonproductiveness, many people have lost possession of what poet Emily Dickinson called this "appetite for silence." In school and at home, among friends and at play, there seem to be ever decreasing opportunities for quiet time apart, as if parents and others have bought into the lie that unless we are always busy, always occupied, always among others, then we are not living fully! And as people grow older and their lives become steadily more hectic and fragmented, they find themselves caught up in a race against time with no time for themselves.

As Anne Morrow Lindbergh has written, "What a commentary on our civilization, when being alone is considered suspect; when one has to apologize for it, make excuses, hide the fact that one practices it — like a secret vice!"

How then do we attain this tranquility in the midst of busy lives, when everything and everyone seems to conspire to intrude upon our solitary time, when it has become increasingly difficult to take a lonely walk or find a deserted path, or spend a quiet evening? We do not necessarily need two years like Thoreau on Walden Pond, or twenty-seven years in a monastery like Trappist monk Thomas Merton, nor do we need to exile ourselves on an island, as did Jean-Jacques Rousseau on Saint Pierre. Jesus was able to withdraw at will, but only for short periods before the world and its demands drew him back. We must find a small, quiet island where we can retreat to rejuvenate and reevaluate. The opportunities are all around us, if we will look for them.

At the center of our town stood my father's Catholic church: a large, oppressively dignified building. Although usually we attended the First Congregational Church across the way, at times St. Mark's captured my imagination. It stood there as a symbol of the unchartered territory, the unknown, "a serious house on serious earth," as the poet Philip Larkin has written. As a young boy I must have spent hours looking at it, but I never approached it: never, that is, until one day when at the age of ten I read a wedding announcement in the local newspaper. So was born an opportunity to satisfy my twin hungers: to see inside the church and to attend a wedding, something I had wanted to do for a couple of years.

I remember the suddenness with which I asked my parents, "Can I go to a wedding?" And I recall just as distinctly their immediate response: "Go ahead!" I also remember my preparations for the big event. I dressed in a pressed white shirt (I learned to iron my clothes as a child) with red bow tie, well-fitted plaid sports coat, dark blue slacks, and black shoes, which had taken me the better part of the evening to polish until they shone like glass.

What do we get nowadays to equal the excitement and the revelation of the "firsts" in those early years? I remember well the missed heartbeat, the appalled glee I felt when I hopped out of my parents' car, climbed the steps, entered cautiously through the open iron doors, and sat down stiffly in the hardwood pew, halfway up the aisle, to gaze in silent awe at the altar and at the stained glass windows. Everyone there must have assumed that I belonged to *someone,* for though an outsider in more ways than one, I felt neither uncomfortable nor unwelcome.

In retrospect, I am sure that my parents waited for me in their car, across the street, but at the time I believed I was fully on my own, and that made all the difference. Since then, my memory has been visited by four pictures that never seem to lose their freshness.

The priest: His voice, manner, and clothes all fascinated me. He was a big man, with a huge dome and dark, heavy-lidded eyes that seemed to stare right through me. Although I felt a little overawed in his presence, he was a very good pastor indeed, for he knew the virtue of brevity.

The groom: He was handsome in his black swallowtail and gray trousers, but his stocky frame and breadth of shoulder belied the nervousness I detected. He looked tired and puffy, though not in any way ill, and I remember wondering, Why isn't he smiling?

Then the bride: As she moved down the aisle, a shaft

of sunlight fell across her body. She wore a simple white dress. A few flowers were twisted in her hair and her whole countenance beamed with smiles. As she passed down the aisle, a breeze wafted through the open windows, and I suddenly became aware of the delicate scent of roses.

Most vivid in my memory: the reception. There were punch and coffee; there were cakes as large as castles. There were a dozen or more pies and fruit bowls over-flowing with grapes. The ice cream, too, was heaped in great fluffy mountains.

But what struck me most of all about the reception was the families. I watched as they got their hands on the food and began to eat it in any order. Cakes, hams, rolls, it didn't matter at all: They merely worked from one plate to the next. And I watched with open mouth as a single, succulent, sizzling sausage was pronged onto the fork of one of the honored guests.

Then flashbulbs popped, and I still wonder what the family members thought when, weeks later, they viewed the photographs and found in several of them a ten-year-old stranger dressed in a blue-gray plaid sports coat, red bow tie, and polished black shoes!

Looking back on all this, one thing is clear to me. My parents showed that they understood the significance of this solitary experience, and this was important, for it meant that other people had allowed me to satisfy a deeply personal curiosity of mine, without needing to explain it or have it explained to me.

Now, years later and married myself, I find I have an ever growing need to make other journeys of solitude, and what's more, my own family has developed a similar inclination. My son, ever since turning five, has more than once said to me, "Daddy, I want to be alone for awhile," or "Can we have some quiet time?" And both my wife and I have learned to create weekly if not daily opportunities to step aside from our busy lives to inquire of their meaning and purpose. Far from being a waste of time, these periods are often exactly what we need to find the energy and inner peace to return to the world and transmit what we have learned. Along with the poet Rainer Maria Rilke, we have discovered the importance of allowing space in our togetherness.

This is not to say that solitude always requires our being alone. Some of our most meaningful times with others have been spent in shared silence while walking along a beach, sitting on the steps, or reading during a quiet evening. With friends, relatives, even strangers — at home, at work, in houses of worship, in business, in marriage, on a crowded city street — we can still retire within ourselves and be immersed in solitude. Indeed, some people seek out crowds so that anonymity can help them feel alone.

One reason I so enjoyed my boyhood is that I lived in a small town surrounded by beautiful countryside. "Every child should have the memory / Of at least one long-after-bedtime walk," wrote poet Robert Frost. Sometimes on a clear night my father would let me stay up later than usual and go outside with him to see the stars. He would sit on the front steps and I would stand between his open legs with my back pressed against his chest, and look up.

Then I would wriggle free from his gentle hold, take a couple of steps away, turn around quickly, and run back into his arms. Over and over I would perform this ritual, until I had dared to go ten, perhaps twelve feet away, then return again to his safe and waiting arms.

One night the air was especially alive with the sounds of crickets. "What's that?" I asked, listening intently.

Remembering a story a friend had told him years before, my father said, "Oh, those are the sounds of the stars twinkling above." The chirping of the crickets and the sound of my father's words are as vivid now as on the night I heard them. It is a tender scene, a moment of peace that I can revisit in my mind.

Recently my own family joined my brother's to drive seven hours to Sequoia National Park, seventy-seven hundred feet above sea level, where we spent four nights. Long drives seem like very short drives when you are sharing them with family members you see only twice a year.

I have always loved the mountains, but this was my first time at Sequoia, and I was completely surprised by its splendor. Stepping out of the car, I suddenly became aware of an immense stillness, as if time had stopped. Sequoias, "kings of their race" as naturalist John Muir called them, towered three hundred feet or more above me, some of them over two thousand years old, a continuous presence, and I exulted.

It's the silence we loved, undisturbed and fully away from everything artificial and commercial and popular. As we walked along the paths, with Ryan and his cousins as our tour guides, the noisy, crowded, competitive environment of the city was out of sight and quickly out of mind. No piped-in electronic "music." No television sets. No radios. No cars. Absolute stillness except for the sound of trees swaying in the breeze or the songs of birds. As I allowed the silence to surround my body, it began to penetrate my soul: unblighted, undemanding, regenerative, refreshing, renewing.

There was tranquility here, conducive to thinking, and praying, and reflecting. And suddenly there flashed to life a scene from my childhood and our own quiet times of contemplation as we picked black raspberries from behind my grandmother's house. We would haul in tiny basketsful and watch as she carefully washed the berries, then put them in a clean bowl, sprinkled sugar over the top layer, and slid them into the refrigerator to be enjoyed after dinner. The sweetness and peace of that memory were somehow akin to what I was feeling as we wandered in the immense forest.

Nighttime at Sequoia gave us an unobstructed view of the sky. My sister-in-law, Betty, an avid astronomer, couldn't contain her excitement as she identified star clouds, nebulae, Sagittarius. I remembered again the quiet times spent with my father's strength and stability to steady me as we gazed at the same stars and I made my tentative forays into the darkness.

"How far can the human eye see?" Betty asked, rhetorically. "It can see 2.9 million light years away," she answered, pointing in the direction of the Andromeda Galaxy, a thick blanket of stars so close that I felt I could reach up and touch them.

Every night we stood in the very presence of a power so incomparable as to make the senses reel. It is a benevolent power, wrote R. Vernon Harris, and those who pay attention will feel, deep within the soul, "a quiet and friendly voice saying: 'This, and so much more also, is yours to share.'" We were looking at God's creation, perfect and breathtaking, and we vaguely understood what we were seeing, and I felt very small but joyfully grateful.

At sunrise we awakened to an intensely blue sky visible through our open windows. We walked, we roamed, we read, we talked, we ate — and we were happy. In that great stillness we reconnected with each other and with something essential inside ourselves. Going out, I understood, was really going in. We became reacquainted with ourselves.

Indeed, whether for reasons of preparation, study, creation, penitence, self-examination, reflection, purification, or prayer — solitude is the most fundamental of all the spiritual disciplines, and we must return to it again and again if we hope to hear the soft voice of inspiration, if we want to function successfully within our family units, if we desire to live fully realized lives. In other words, in order to strengthen our connections with others, we sometimes need to be by ourselves.

I am grateful to my parents not only for creating the space that enabled me to pursue the joys of solitude, but also for teaching me that no journey is more exciting, more adventurous, and more revealing than the journey within.

Education, reading, integrity, prayer, solitude: All of these values fit under the category of living wisely. And if there is one overall reason for the value of the family, if there is one overall aspiration for parents, it is to teach children to do just that.

Aristotle called wisdom "the greatest good." Scripture tells us that wisdom is more precious than rubies, more important than longevity or riches or honor. Proverbs 3:18 likens it to a "tree of life to those who lay hold of her"; and its author, Solomon, said that his writings are intended for "gaining instruction in wise dealing, righteousness, justice, and equity," and also for teaching "shrewdness to the simple, knowledge and prudence to the young" (1:3–4). Wisdom begins with a fear of the Lord; its "end and aim," says the Talmud, "is repentance and good deeds."

If our children don't see such wisdom practiced at home, it is unlikely they will see it anywhere else.

CONCLUSION

That return visit to my hometown of Amherst, Massachusetts, after a thirty-five year absence brought back so many childhood memories with such force and clarity that it seemed almost imperative to write about some of them — and so I have. This journey has been deeply satisfying for me and, I hope, for the reader.

Like most families, ours loved to tell stories. All of my grandparents, especially, had a treasure trove of folktales and sagas about families — ours and others — to relate to us, and many of these have stayed with my brother and me over the years — to be retold to our own children. I vividly recall one favorite story, whose source is unknown, that my paternal grandmother told me when I was about ten years old.

One day my nine-year-old brother wanted to play with our grandfather, but he needed at least two hours of time alone to complete his work for the day. So he devised a clever game to keep his grandson happily entertained. From a magazine he cut a multicolored picture of the world, tore it into dozens of pieces, scattered them on the living room carpet, and said, "Put the pieces together, like a jigsaw puzzle — and when you've finished that, we'll play!" Then he set a timer for two hours and retreated to his study where he settled into his work.

Fifteen minutes later there was a quiet knock at the door. He opened it to find his grandson standing there, smiling broadly.

"Grandpa, I did it!" he exclaimed. "I put the world together!"

"Impossible," grandfather said, with a chuckle. "How could you have done it so quickly?" In disbelief, grandfather took my brother's hand, they walked into the living room, and there, sure enough, lay the same picture of the world.

"How did you do that?" grandfather asked, incredulous. "It would have taken me much longer!"

In answer my brother began to turn over the pieces of

the world. And when he had finished, there on the other side was the portrait of a mother, a father, and their three children.

"You see, Grandpa, I put the family together first, and then the whole world came together!"

I have been thinking about this story for a long time. The world we see today is an increasingly secular and fragmented, sometimes dangerous and coldly daunting place. Technology, changing values, and competition for our time and energies, wrote Henri J. M. Nouwen, make it hard to avoid completely the forces that distance us from "our innermost selves, our fellow human beings, and our God." America, said Mother Teresa, is a lonely country. And yet people everywhere yearn to be connected, to be affirmed, to overcome a gnawing dissatisfaction with life in general.

How, then, do we bring our world together? In large part, by returning to the institution upon which all societies are founded: the family. And how do we transform the family, which in many ways seems so beset with problems? By approaching in prayer and with all humility its Creator, and He will show us the way. As 2 Chronicles 7:14 tells us, "If my people who are called by my name humble themselves, pray, seek my face, and turn from their wicked ways, then I will hear from heaven, and will forgive their sin and heal their land." It is as simple, and as profound, as that.

For although the conditions of modern life seem to

make the quest for a happy family more difficult than ever before, we must remember that we serve a God of new beginnings. He has made us complete. He strengthens us and fulfills our needs. He has granted to us everything we require for living in holy relation with Him. It is never too late to start over. It is always within our power to change.

Throughout this book I have referred to the Bible, which is for me *the* book on family, because it really explains what is expected of me as God's servant and as a husband and a father, a son and a friend. My childhood home was spiritually rich because so much of what we did — and thought — found its origin in the Bible's commandments, and in their explanations in the Bible's stories and commentaries on them. In these narratives and other spiritual readings, my grandparents and parents found reasons for the existence of their families and guidance on how to strengthen them. And now, so do I.

God made the world, revealed His will to humanity, and promised redemption to those who follow that will. He is universal and moral, an intensely personal God not only of judgment but of compassion, goodness, tenderness, care, and love. Submit to God, fear Him, trust Him, obey Him: These precepts are not abstractions but practical rules intended for every parent and child, every relation and neighbor. In strengthening our connection to God, we will strengthen our connection to others.

Human life is also sacred, created in the image of God. Because we have been given free will, we are responsible and ultimately accountable for what we say and what we do, and there are rewards and consequences for moral behavior or misbehavior. "What is hateful to you," said the great Rabbi Hillel, "do not do unto your neighbor." In this regard, Albert Einstein speaks for everybody when he says in "My Credo":

> We are here for the sake of others.... Above all, for those upon whose smile and well-being our own happiness depends, and also for the countless unknown souls with whose fate we are connected by a bond of sympathy. Many times a day I realize how much my own outer and inner life is built upon the labors of my fellow men, both living and dead, and how earnestly I must exert myself in order to give in return as much as I have received.

Indeed, life is not a dress rehearsal. What we do and say today will become tomorrow's memories. "We have only one life — so quick, so fast," said the anonymous poet. "What good is done in this life, will last."

Our families are our legacies, the record and result of the choices we make. May it be that someday, someone will say of this generation's families, "It is good that they passed this way. I am better because they were here."

*I*f in any of the following notes the title alone is listed, then full bibliographic information may be found either in an earlier citation or in the Recommended Reading list. Every effort has been made to credit all sources, but if any have been inadvertently overlooked the publishers will be pleased to make the necessary arrangement at the first opportunity.

introduction

xi   Thomas Carlyle (1795–1881), English poet, essayist. "Signs of the Times" (1829) in his *Sartor Resartus and Selected Prose* (New York: Holt, Rinehart and Winston, 1970), pp. 3–29.

xii   James Q. Wilson, *The Wall Street Journal,* August 22, 1994.

xiii   Philosophers: See for example Alfred North Whitehead (1861–1947), English logician best known for his work in mathematical logic. Quoted by American civil rights leader Martin Luther King, Jr. (1929–1964) in *Where Do We Go from Here: Chaos or Community?* (New York: Harper and Row, 1967), p. 169.

xv–xvi   Mother Teresa [Agnes Gonxha Bojaxhiu] (1910–1997), founder of Sisters of Charity, Calcutta, and Nobel Prize winner. *A Simple Path,* compiled by Lucinda Vardey (New York: Ballantine, 1995), p. 79.

xvi   The teachings of Confucius (c. 551–479 B.C.), generally recognized as China's greatest sage, are enshrined in *The Analects.* I have used David Hinton's translation (Washington, D.C.: Counterpoint, 1998), pp. xx, 229–32.

xvi   See *The Desert Fathers,* translated by Helen Waddell (Ann Arbor: The University of Michigan Press, 1957).

chapter 1: the need for connections

1   Simone Weil (1909–43), French essayist and philosopher. Quoted by internationally noted psychologist and author Mary Pipher (1950–) in her *Another Country: Navigating the Emotional Terrain of Our Elders,* p. 59.

2   V[idiadhar] S[urajprasad] Naipaul, (1932–), Trinidad-born English novelist. *A Way in the World* (New York: Knopf, 1994), p. 11.

2   Michel Eyquem de Montaigne (1533–1592), French essayist. Quoted by François Jacob in his *The Logic of Life: A History of Heredity* (Princeton, N.J.: Princeton University Press, 1993), p. 20.

5–6   C. S. Lewis (1898–1963), British critic, poet, Christian polemicist, science-fiction novelist, scholar. *Surprised by Joy: The Shape of My Early Life* (New York: Harcourt, Brace and World, 1955), pp. 15, 16.

7   Graham Greene (1904–1991), English novelist, dramatist. *The Power and the Glory* (New York: Bantam, 1954), part 1, chapter 1, p. 7.

9   Thomas Moore (1940–), a leading writer in North America and in Europe in the areas of archetypal psychology, mythology and the arts.

Soul Mates: Honoring the Mysteries of Love and Relationship, pp. 129–30.

10 Erich Fromm (1900–1980), German neo-Freudian who forged a link between psychoanalysis and social psychology. See *Escape from Freedom* (New York: Holt, Rinehart and Winston, 1941), pp. 25–32; and *You Should Be as Gods* (Greenwich, Conn.: Fawcett, 1966), pp. 37–71.

10 William Wordsworth (1770–1850), English poet. "Lines Composed a Few Miles above Tintern Abbey" (1798) in *Wordsworth: Poems* (New York: Knopf, 1995), p. 50, line 91.

14 St. John of the Cross (1542–91), one of the greatest figures in the history of Western mysticism. See "The Dark Night" in *The Collected Works of St. John of the Cross,* translated by Kieran Kavanaugh and Otilio Rodriguez (Garden City, N.Y.: Doubleday, 1964), pp. 363–65. For a concise overview of this experience, see Richard J. Foster's *Celebration of Discipline: The Path to Spiritual Growth,* pp. 89–92.

chapter 2: to care for the old

17 Philo [Judaeus] of Alexandria (c. 20 B.C.–c. A.D. 50), the most important Hellenistic Jew of his age, a prolific author of philosophical and exegetical writings. See the commentary on the fifth commandment ("Honor your father and mother") in his treatise, "On the Ten Commandments" in *The Works of Philo: Complete and Unabridged: III,* translated by Charles Duke Yonge (London: Henry G. Bohn, 1855), pp. 162–63.

18 Albert Schweitzer (1875–1965), German theologian and physician, 1952 Nobel Prize winner. Quoted by Rabbi Laureate Harold S. Kushner (1932–) of Temple Israel in Natick, Mass. in *How Good Do We Have to Be?,* p. 157.

20 Rabbi Joseph Telushkin (1948–), scholar, spiritual leader of the Synagogue for the Performing Arts in Los Angeles. *Jewish Wisdom: Ethical, Spiritual and Historical Lessons from the Great Works and Thinkers,* p. 251.

20–21 Of help to me in understanding the complicated relationship between parent and child is Rabbi Harold S. Kushner's *How Good Do We Have to Be?,* pp. 66–95.

21–22   The Confucian scholar is quoted by Alfons Deeken, S.J. in *Growing Old and How to Cope with It* (San Francisco: Ignatius Press, 1972), p. 5.

28   Emily Dickinson (1830–1896), American poet. *The Letters of Emily Dickinson, Vol. I,* edited by Thomas H. Johnson and Theodora V. W. Ward (Cambridge, Mass.: Harvard University Press, 1958), pp. 305–306. Quoted by Dale Salwak in *The Wonders of Solitude* (Novato, Calif.: New World Library, 1998), p. 102.

33   Rainer Maria Rilke (1875–1926), German poet, essayist. "The Poet" in *Selected Poems,* translated by Albert Ernest Flemming (New York: Routledge, 1983, 1985, 1990), p. 71, lines 5–8.

33   Mary Pipher, *Another Country: Navigating the Emotional Terrain of Our Elders,* p. 11.

35   The heart of Judaism is a tradition of words whose sources have been likened to an inverted pyramid. At the base is the Bible — "the words of the living God" — made up of the Law (Torah or five books of Moses), the Prophets (Nevi'im), and the Writings (Ketuvim), all recorded over a period of more than 1,300 years. From this powerful base the tradition expands outward to include the scholarly interpretations in the Oral Torah or Talmud (comprising the Mishnah and the Gemara). See Dale Salwak's *The Wisdom of Judaism* (Novato, Calif.: New World Library, 1997).

35   F[rederick] E[rnest] Crowe (1915–), Jesuit priest and professor of philosophy and theology at various universities. Quoted by Alfons Deeken, S.J. in *Growing Old and How to Cope with It,* p. 11.

35   Norman Cousins (1912–1993), American essayist, editor. See his "Foreword" to Pat York's *Going Strong* (New York: Little, Arcade/Little, Brown, 1991), p. 10.

36   Christopher Lasch (1939–1994), American sociologist, former professor of history at the University of Rochester. *The Culture of Narcissism: American Life in an Age of Diminishing Expectations* (New York: Norton, 1979, 1991).

40   Aristotle (384–322 B.C.), Greek philosopher and disciple of Plato. "*Poetics:* 13. The Tragic Hero" in *The Pocket Aristotle,* edited by Justin D. Kaplan, translated by Ingram Bywater (New York: Washington Square Press, 1958), p. 357.

40   James [Allen] Michener (1907–1997), American writer. *The World Is My Home* (New York: Random House, 1992). p. 297.

41   Rabbi David J. Wolpe (1958–), senior rabbi of Sinai Temple in Los
      Angeles. *Making Loss Matter: Creating Meaning in Difficult Times,*
      p. 112.

42   Norman Cousins, "Foreword," *Going Strong,* p. 11.

43   Robert Browning (1812–1889), English poet. See "Rabbi Ben Ezra" in
      Dramatis Personae (1864), quoted from *The Selected Poetry of Robert
      Browning* (New York: Modern Library, 1951), p. 479, stanza 1,
      lines 1–2.

chapter 3: hearts undivided

45   George Eliot [Mary Anne Evans] (1819–80), English novelist.
      Adam Bede (New York: Washington Square Press, 1956), chapter 54,
      p. 523.

45   Martin Luther (1483–1546), founder of the German Reformation.
      See "On Married Life" (1522) in *The Table Talk of Martin Luther,*
      translated and edited by William Hazlitt (London: G. Bell and
      Sons, 1878).

46   William C. Bennett (1943–), codirector of Empower America. *The
      Moral Compass: Stories for a Life's Journey* (New York: Simon and
      Schuster, 1995), p. 483.

46   Rabbi Harold S. Kushner, *How Good Do We Have to Be? A New
      Understanding of Guilt and Forgiveness,* p. 115.

47   John Donne (1572–1631), English poet and divine. "To Sir Henry
      Wotton" (1597–1598) in *The Complete Poetry of John Donne,* edited by
      John T. Shawcross (Garden City, N.Y.: Doubleday, 1967), p. 195, line 1.

48   Philip Larkin (1922–1985), English poet, essayist, novelist.
      "Aubade" in *Collected Poems,* edited by Anthony Thwaite (New
      York: Farrar, Straus and Giroux, 1989), p. 209, line 50.

58   Robert Frost, (1874–1963), American poet. "Nothing Gold Can Stay"
      in *The Poetry of Robert Frost,* edited by Edward Connery Lathem
      (New York: Holt, Rinehart and Winston, 1969), p. 223, line 8.

59   Carl Gustav Jung (1875–1961), Swiss psychiatrist, developed theory
      of "collective unconscious." *Two Essays on Analytical Psychology*
      (1928; New York: Meridian, 1956), p. 193.

59   Rainer Maria Rilke, *Letters to a Young Poet,* translated by Joan M.
      Burnham (Novato, Calif.: New World Library, 1992), p. 65.

59   Anne Morrow Lindbergh (1906–), wife of the late Charles Lindbergh, memoirist, essayist. *Dearly Beloved: A Theme and Variations* (New York: Harcourt, Brace and World, 1962), pp. 114, 115.

60–61   "This, too, will [shall] pass away": first used by Abraham Lincoln in an address to the Wisconsin State Agricultural Society (September 30, 1859) in which he said of the aphorism: "How much it expresses! How chastening in the hour of pride! How consoling in the depths of affliction!" The *Random House Dictionary of Popular Proverbs and Sayings,* edited by Gregory Titelman (New York: Random House, 1996), p. 335, attributes it to King Solomon: "A Sultan asked Solomon to develop a sentence which would be visible at any time, and which would be true and appropriate in both adverse and prosperous times." The consoling dictum comes close to that of Julian of Norwich which my grandparents used often: "All shall be well."

63   [Nelle] Harper Lee (1926–), American writer. *To Kill a Mockingbird* (New York: Warner Books, 1960), chapter 3, p. 30.

63   Father Thomas Keating (1937–), Cistercian monk and priest and a founder of the Centering Prayer movement and Contemplation Outreach. See *The Mystery of Christ: The Liturgy as Spiritual Expression* (New York: Continuum, 1997), pp. 93–121; and *The Contemplative Journey, Volume 2: Study Guide* (Snowmass, Colo.: St. Benedict's Monastery, 1997).

chapter 4: a child's innocence

65   Elizabeth [Anne] Chase Akers (1832–1911), American journalist, poet. "Rock Me to Sleep, Mother" (1860). Quoted in *Leonard and Thelma Spinrad's Speaker's Lifetime Library* (West Nyack, N.Y.: Parker Publishing, 1979), pp. 51, 237.

72   Korney Ivanovich Chukovsky [Nikolay Vasilyevich Korneychukov] (1882–1969), Russian literary critic, language theorist, translator, and author of children's books; often called the first modern Russian writer for children. See his classic study of the language of children, *From Two to Five,* translated and edited by Miriam Morton (1933; Berkeley: University of California Press, 1963, 1968).

72–73   Douglas Jerrold (1803–1857), English satirist. Quoted by John

M[ummau] Drescher in *If I Were Starting My Family Again* (Nashville, Tenn.: Abingdon, 1979), p. 21.

74–76   Bruno Bettelheim (1903–1990), holocaust survivor noted for his work with autistic children, former Professor of Education and of both Psychology and Psychiatry at the University of Chicago. *The Uses of Enchantment: The Meaning and Importance of Fairy Tales* (New York: Knopf, 1976), pp. 309–10.

75, 81–82 Plato (c. 427–348 B.C.), the great Greek philosopher and pupil of Socrates. The passages come from Books II and III of Plato's *The Republic,* in which Socrates argues that education begins in the nursery, with fables and fairy stories. These he says must be carefully censored to ensure a suitable moral tone. In Book III, he says that literature must deal only with suitable subjects, and only in a suitable manner. A noble art, purified of unwholesomeness and extravagance, will develop in the young the characteristics of nobility.

76   John M[ummau] Drescher (1928–), together with his wife, Betty, conducts family and married couples retreats throughout the U.S. and Canada. *If I Were Starting My Family Again,* p. 47.

77   Allan Bloom (1930–1992), American educator. *The Closing of the American Mind* (New York: Simon and Schuster, 1987), pp. 58–59.

78   Margaret Mead (1901–1978), renowned anthropologist. Referred to in Neil Postman's *The Disappearance of Childhood* (New York: Random House, 1982, 1994), p. 150. See also Mead's *Culture and Commitment: A Study of the Generation Gap* (Garden City, N.Y.: Doubleday, 1970), which Postman discusses on pages 89–90.

chapter 5: betrayal of trust

91   Francis Thompson (1859–1907), English poet, essayist. *The Text of "The Hound of Heaven,"* edited by John F. Quinn (Chicago: Loyola University Press, 1970), line 15, p. 9.

93   Euripides (c. 480–406 B.C.), Greek dramatist. *The Suppliant Woman* (c. 421 B.C.), translated by Rosanna Warren and Stephen Scully (New York: Oxford University Press, 1995). In lines 1071–73 (p. 59), the Chorus says: "What greater grief can there be / for mortals, than to see / our own children, ash and bone."

95–96   Ronald [Wilson] Reagan (1911–) [with Richard G. Hubler], fortieth

American president. *Where's the Rest of Me? The Autobiography of Ronald Reagan* (New York: Karz Publishers, 1965, 1981), pp. 7–8.

98   Jean Piaget (1896–1980), Swiss-born researcher in developmental psychology and genetic epistemology. See *The Child's Concept of the World* (New York: Harcourt, Brace, 1929); *The Origins of Intelligence in Children* (New York: International University Press, 1952); and *The Construction of Reality in the Child* (New York: Basic Books, 1954).

99   Stephen L. Carter (1954–), the William Nelson Cromwell Professor of Law at Yale. He paraphrases Margaret Farley in *Integrity*, p. 142.

102   Arnold Toynbee (1889–), English historian. *Man's Concern with Death* (St. Louis: McGraw-Hill, 1968), p. 271.

102   Arthur Miller (1915–), American dramatist whose works are concerned with the responsibility of each individual to other members of society. *After the Fall: A Play in Two Acts* (1964; New York: Penguin, 1980), act 2, lines 23–24, p. 104.

103   Kay Redfield Jamison (1951–), professor of psychiatry at the Johns Hopkins University School of Medicine. *Night Falls Fast: Understanding Suicide*, pp. 291–92.

110   Mitch Albom (1958–), writer for the *Detroit Free Press. Tuesdays with Morrie: An Old Man, a Young Man, and Life's Greatest Lesson*, p. 91.

110   W. H. Auden (1907–1973), English-born American poet. "September 1, 1939" in *The English Auden: Poems, Essays & Dramatic Writings 1927–39*, edited by Edward Mendelson (London and Boston: Faber and Faber, 1977), p. 245, line 88.

111   Leo Tolstoy (1828–1910), Russian novelist. *The Kingdom of God Is within You*, translated by Aylmer Maude (London: Oxford University Press, 1936), p. 136.

111   Johann Wolfgang von Goethe (1749–1832), German-born writer who profoundly influenced the growth of literary romanticism. "Before the City Gate" in *Goethe's Faust: Part I*, translated by Walter Kaufmann (1808–1832; New York: Doubleday, 1961), p. 145, lines 3–4.

111   Robert Louis Stevenson (1850–1894), English novelist. In *The Strange Case of Dr. Jekyll and Mr. Hyde* (New York: Dutton, 1925), Stevenson explores the theme of man's double nature.

111   Carl Gustav Jung, *Modern Man in Search of a Soul*, translated by W. S. Dell and Cary F. Baynes (New York: Harcourt, Brace, 1933), pp. 11, 260–62.

chapter 6: the family of god

113   Oliver Wendell Holmes, Jr. (1809–1894), American physician, writer. See Eleanor M. Tilton, *Amiable Autocrat: A Biography of Dr. Oliver Wendell Holmes* (New York: Henry Schuman, 1947), p. 252.

114–15 St. Augustine of Hippo (354–430), *Confessions* (397–401), translated by F[rank] J. Sheed (New York: Sheed and Ward, 1943), book I, section I, p. 3.

126   Ronald Blythe (1922–), English literary critic. *Characters and Their Landscapes* (San Diego: Harcourt Brace Jovanovich, 1983), p. 60.

131   Victor Hugo (1802–1885), French poet, novelist, playwright. "Fantine" in *Les Misérables,* translated by Lee Fabnestock and Norman MacAfee (New York: Penguin, 1987), book V, chapter IV, p. 167.

132   Mother Teresa, *A Simple Path,* pp. xxxii, 79.

133   St. Augustine, *Confessions,* book 13, section 1, p. 321.

134   Henri J. M. Nouwen (1932–1996), ordained Roman Catholic priest. *Our Greatest Gift* (New York: HarperCollins, 1994), p. 67.

chapter 7: the gift of love

135   Mother Teresa, *A Simple Path,* p. 87.

136   Robert Frost, "The Death of the Hired Man" in *The Poetry of Robert Frost,* p. 38, line 118.

139   Henri J. M. Nouwen, *Beyond the Mirror: Reflections on Death and Life* (New York: Crossroad, 1991), p. 51.

143–145 Fulton J. Sheen (1895–1979), American Roman Catholic archbishop who, through the broadcast media, became the most prominent spokesman for the Roman Catholic Church in the U.S. *God Love You* (Garden City, N.Y.: Doubleday, 1981), pp. 183, 169, 193.

146   Thomas Merton (1915–1968), French-born American Trappist monk, author. Quoted by Henri J. M. Nouwen in "The Desert Counsel to Flee the World," *Sojourners* 9 (June 1980): 15.

146   Carl Sandburg (1878–1967), American poet, essayist, biographer. The quoted passage comes from a letter to his sister, Mary, dated October 13, 1904, and now held at the University of Illinois. It is referred to by Penelope Niven in her *Carl Sandburg: A Biography* (New York: Charles Scribner's Sons, 1991), p. 93. "Happiness," Sandburg adds, "has its source in the soul, in individuality."

152   The first quote from Mother Teresa appears in *No Greater Love,* p. 132. The second appears in Navin Chawla's *Mother Teresa* (Rockport, Maine: Element Books, 1992), p. xxiv.

chapter 8: family unity

153   Douglas Dunn (1942–), Scottish poet. "Disenchantment" in *Dante's Drum-kit* (London and Boston: Faber and Faber, 1993), pp. 46, IX, line 67.

153   Peter J. Gomes (1939–), professor of Christian morals and minister of the Memorial Church, Harvard. *The Good Book: Reading the Bible with Mind and Heart* (New York: William Morrow, 1996), p. 213.

164   Robert Coles (1929–), American psychiatrist, educator, and author, specializing in child psychology. *Anna Freud: The Dream of Psychoanalysis* (Reading, Mass.: Addison-Wesley, 1992), p. 20.

164–67   Duong Van Mai Elliott (1941–), Vietnamese-born author. *The Sacred Willow: Four Generations in the Life of a Vietnamese Family* (New York: Oxford University Press, 1999), pp. xiii, 474.

chapter 9: the value of family

171   Stephen L. Carter, *Civility: Manners, Morals, and the Etiquette of Democracy,* p. 229.

172   Will Durant (1885–1981) [with Ariel Durant]. American author and Pulitzer Prize-winning historian. *A Dual Autobiography* (New York: Simon and Schuster, 1977), p. 127.

172   George Santayana (1863–1952), Spanish-born American philosopher and critic. "Reason in Society, Chapter 2: 'The Family in Society'" (1905–1906) in *The Life of Reason* (Amherst, N.Y.: Prometheus, 1998), p. 104.

174   Henri J. M. Nouwen, *Reaching Out: The Three Movements of the Spiritual Life* (Garden City, N.Y.: Doubleday, 1975), p. 58.

174   Jean [Johann] Paul Richter (1763–1825), German romantic novelist. Quoted in *The New Dictionary of Thoughts,* edited by C. N. Catrevas et al (New York: Standard Book, 1966), p. 307.

175   James Hillman (1926–), Jungian analyst and originator of the post-Jungian "archetypal psychology." *The Soul's Code: In Search of Character and Calling,* p. 83.

179   Robert Frost, "The Road Not Taken" in *The Poetry of Robert Frost,* p. 105, lines 16–20.

179   William James (1842–1910), American philosopher. *The Will to Believe and Other Essays in Popular Philosophy* (1897; New York: Charles Scribner's Sons, 1956), p. 31.

182   Alfred Edward Newton (1863–1940), American bibliophile. *The Amenities of Book-Collecting and Kindred Affections* (Boston: Atlantic Monthly Press, 1918). Quoted by Otto L. Bettmann in *The Delights of Reading* (Boston: David R. Godine, 1987), p. 49.

182–83   Eudora Welty (1909–), American novelist, short fiction writer. *One Writer's Beginnings* (Cambridge, Mass.: Harvard University Press, 1984), pp. 5–6.

184–85   Gail Sheehy (1937–), political editor and contributor to *Vanity Fair* in which she writes extended analyses of American and world leaders. *The Man Who Changed the World: The Lives of Mikhail S. Gorbachev* (New York: HarperCollins, 1990), p. 245.

185–86   James Baldwin (1924–1987), African-American author and civil rights advocate. Quoted by Otto L. Bettman in *The Delights of Reading,* p. 37.

186–87   Anna Quindlen (1951–), American novelist. *How Reading Changed My Life* (New York: Ballantine, 1998), p. 9.

187–88   Maya Angelou (1928–), celebrated African-American writer; Reynolds Professor at Wake Forest University. *I Know Why the Caged Bird Sings* (New York: Bantam, 1971, 1993), pp. 53, 14, 100.

187   William Shakespeare, "Sonnet 29" in *The Sonnets,* edited by William Burto (New York: New American Library, 1964), p. 69, line 1.

188   Roald Dahl (1916–1990), popular children's author. *Matilda* (New York: Viking, 1988).

188–89   Isaac Stern (1920–) [with Chaim Potok], American violinist. *My First 79 Years* (New York: Knopf, 1999), p. 89.

190   Jack Miles (1942–), former Jesuit, studied at Pontifical Gregorian College, Rome, and the Hebrew University, Jerusalem; holds a doctorate in Near Eastern languages from Harvard. *God: A Biography* (New York: Knopf, 1995), p. 120.

191   United States Senate Chaplain Dr. Lloyd John Ogilvie (1930–) spoke at the Fork Union Military Academy's 100th anniversary service. The quote comes from the Academy's *Religious Herald,* October 29, 1998, p. 2.

192   Plato, *The Republic,* Book II.

193-94   Stephen L. Carter, *Integrity*, p. 7.

195   Rabbi David J. Wolpe, "Why the Silence about God?," *Los Angeles Times,* 19 December 1993, p. 5. His *Teaching Your Children about God: A Modern Jewish Approach* (New York: HarperCollins, 1993, 1995) is a splendid guide to explaining God to children from ages four to fourteen.

196   Martin Luther King, Jr., *Where Do We Go from Here: Chaos or Community?,* p. 171.

196   Carl Gustav Jung, *The Development of Personality* (Princeton, N.J.: Princeton University Press, 1974), pp. 182-84. "One of the great problems of mankind," he writes, "is that we suffer from a poverty of the spirit which stands in glaring contrast to our scientific and technological advance." See also his *Civilization in Transition* (Princeton, N.J.: Princeton University Press, 1975).

196   Pierre Teilhard de Chardin (1881-1955), French Roman Catholic priest, geologist, philosopher-theologian. *The Divine Milieu: An Essay on the Interior Life* (1957; New York: Harper and Row, 1960, 1965). See also his *The Future of Man,* translated by Norman Denny (1959; New York: Harper and Row, 1964).

196   Thomas Moore, *Soul Mates: Honoring the Mysteries of Love and Relationship,* p. 148.

197   Sir Isaac Newton (1642-1727), English mathematician and physicist. Quoted by Dale Salwak in *The Power of Prayer* (Novato, Calif.: New World Library, 1998), p. xii.

197   St. Augustine of Hippo is quoted by Richard J. Foster in *Prayer: Finding the Heart's True Home* (San Francisco: HarperCollins, 1992), p. 1.

197   St. Jean Marie Baptiste Vianney (1786-1869), France's curé d'arts, canonized 1925. Quoted by Richard J. Foster in *Prayer: Finding the Heart's True Home,* p. 27.

198   George Matheson (1842-1906), hymn lyricist, preacher. For the circumstances surrounding the writing of the hymn "O Love That Wilt Not Let Me Go" (1882), see Donald Macmillan's *Life of George Matheson* (New York: A. C. Armstrong and Sons, 1907).

198   A[iden] W[ilson] Tozer (1897-1963), *The Pursuit of God* (Wheaton, Ill.: Tyndale House, 1949), p. 11.

199   St. Frances de Sales (1567-1622), bishop of Geneva and one of the

leaders of the Counter-Revolution. *Introduction to the Devout Life,* translated by John K. Ryan (New York: Doubleday, 1955), p. 84.

200, 203 An inspiring collection of Mother Teresa's teachings on prayer may be found in *Everything Starts from Prayer: Mother Teresa's Meditations on Spiritual Life for People of All Faiths.* See also *No Greater Love,* pp. 3–34; and *A Simple Path,* pp. 3–38.

202 Philip Zaleski, "The Life of Spiritual Combat: An Interview with Abbot Hugh Gilbert" in *Parabola: Myth, Tradition, and the Search for Meaning* 24 (May 1999): 14.

204 Abbot Dom MacDonald is quoted by Frank Bianco in *Voices of Silence: Lives of the Trappists Today* (New York: Paragon House, 1991), p. 104.

204 "The family that prays together": According to the *Random House Dictionary of Popular Proverbs and Sayings* (p. 96), this aphorism was originated by commercial writer Al Scalpone and used as a motto of the Roman Catholic Rosary Crusade by Father Patrick Peyton. It first appeared in print in the 3 April 1948 issue of *St. Joseph Magazine* (Oregon).

204–05 Henry David Thoreau (1817–1862), American philosopher, naturalist, essayist. *Walden,* edited by J. Lyndon Shanley (Princeton, N.J.: Princeton University Press, 1971), p. 90.

206 Emily Dickinson is quoted from one of her letters by John Evangelist Walsh in his *The Hidden Life of Emily Dickinson* (New York: Simon and Schuster, 1971), p. 218.

206 Anne Morrow Lindbergh, *Gift from the Sea* (New York: Random House, 1991), p. 50.

207 Philip Larkin, "Church Going," *Collected Poems,* p. 98, line 55.

210 In *Letters to a Young Poet,* Rainer Maria Rilke defines marriage as being "comprised of two lonelinesses protecting one another, setting limits, and acknowledging one another" (p. 72).

210 Robert Frost, "The Fear" in *The Poetry of Robert Frost,* p. 92, lines 82–83.

211 John Muir (1838–1914), explorer, scientist, and author who helped to establish the modern conservation movement. *John Muir in His Own Words: A Book of Quotations,* compiled and edited by Peter Browning (Lafayette, Calif.: Great West Books, 1988), p. 54, #245.

213 R. Vernon Harris (1911–), American religious writer. Quoted by Dale Salwak in *The Wonders of Solitude,* p. 58.

214   Aristotle, "Nichomachean Ethics" in *The Pocket Aristotle,* books I
       and II, pp. 160–97.

conclusion

215   Antoine de Saint-Exupéry (1900–1944), French writer and aviator.
       The Little Prince, translated by Richard Howard (1943; San Diego:
       Harcourt, 1971, 2000), chapter 21, p. 63.
217   Henri J. M. Nouwen, *Making All Things New: An Invitation to the
       Spiritual Life* (San Francisco: Harper and Row, 1981), pp. 35–36.
217   Mother Teresa, *A Simple Path,* p. 95.
218   On our power to change, see the Monks of New Skete (editors), *In
       the Spirit of Happiness* (Boston: Little, Brown, 1999), pp. 48–67.
219   Rabbi Hillel (c. 70 B.C.–A.D. 10), Jewish rabbi and teacher, the first
       scholar to systematize the interpretation of Scriptural Law. Quoted
       by Rabbi Joseph Telushkin in *Jewish Literacy: The Most Important
       Things to Know about the Jewish Religion, Its People, and Its History*
       (New York: William Morrow, 1991), pp. 120–22.
219   Albert Einstein (1879–1955), German-born American physicist and
       Nobel laureate. He delivered "My Credo" for the German League
       of Human Rights, 1932. The full text is reprinted in Dale Salwak's
       The Wisdom of Judaism (Novato, Calif.: New World Library, 1997),
       pp. 127–28. See also Alice Calaprice's *The Quotable Einstein*
       (Princeton, N.J.: Princeton University Press, 1996), p. 107; and
       Henry J. Leach's *Living Philosophies: A Series of Intimate Credos*
       (New York: Simon and Schuster, 1931), p. 3.
219   "What we do and say...": For this insight I am grateful to Dr.
       Lloyd John Ogilvie, who has preached and written often on the
       theme of the preciousness of time.

LIST OF ILLUSTRATIONS

---

chapter 1: the need for connections

On my mother's lap, aged seven, with my father and brother Glenn (1954).

chapter 2: to care for the old

Peasants in Van Dinh, Vietnam, whose families still remember Mai Elliott's great-grandfather Duong Lam. Photo taken 1993. (Photo courtesy of Duong Van Mai Elliott.)

chapter 3: hearts undivided

My parent's wedding day, June 3, 1944, with matron of honor Stashya Salwak and best man Joe Salwak.

chapter 4: a child's innocence

My wife's mother, Martie, at four years old with her brother, Ben, and cousin, Richard, taken by their home at Trinidad, Colorado.

chapter 5: betrayal of trust

Photo courtesy of Comstock Images.

chapter 6: the family of god

Photo courtesy of Comstock Images.

chapter 7: the gift of love

David at the hospice, Christmas 1995, with his sisters Betty (left) and Douglass.

chapter 8: family unity

Mai and David Elliott, with her family in front of her parents' house in Saigon, Tet 1966. First row: niece Lily. Second row: father, first from left; Mai, second from left; sister Tuyet, third from left; Mai's mother is in the second row, far right. David is in the last row, first from left. (Photo courtesy of Duong Van Mai Elliott)

chapter 9: the value of family

Fiftieth wedding anniversary picture of my parents along with their sons and family.

RECOMMENDED READING

Albom, Mitch. *Tuesdays with Morrie: An Old Man, a Young Man, and Life's Greatest Lesson.* New York: Doubleday, 1997.

Breggin, Peter R. *Reclaiming Our Children: A Healing Plan for a Nation in Crisis.* Cambridge, Mass.: Perseus Books, 2000.

Brother Lawrence [Nicholas Herman]. *The Practice of the Presence of God.* Oxford, England: Oneworld, 1999.

Carter, Jimmy. *The Virtues of Aging.* New York: Ballantine, 1998.

Carter, Stephen L. *Civility: Manners, Morals, and the Etiquette of Democracy.* New York: Basic Books, 1998.

———. *Integrity.* New York: Basic Books, 1996.

Ezzo, Gary, and Anne Marie Ezzo. *Growing Kids God's Way: Biblical Ethics for Parenting.* Simi Valley, Calif.: Micah 6:8 Publishers, 1998.

Fine, Aubrey H. *Fathers and Sons: Bridging the Generations.* Dubuque, Iowa: Kendall/Hunt, 2000.

Foster, Richard J. *Celebration of Discipline: The Path to Spiritual Growth.* San Francisco: Harper & Row, 1978.

Heald, Cynthia. *When the Father Holds You Close: A Journey to Deeper Intimacy with God.* Nashville, Tenn.: Thomas Nelson, 1999.

Hillman, James. *The Soul's Code: In Search of Character and Calling.* New York: Random House, 1996.

Hinckley, Gordon B. *Standing for Something: 10 Neglected Virtues That Will Heal Our Hearts and Homes.* New York: Random House, 2000.

Jamison, Kay Redfield. *Night Falls Fast: Understanding Suicide.* New York: Knopf, 1999.

Kushner, Rabbi Harold S. *How Good Do We Have to Be? A New Understanding of Guilt and Forgiveness.* Boston: Little Brown, 1996.

Lewis, Robert. *Real Family Values: Leading Your Family into the Twenty-First Century with Clarity and Conviction.* Sisters, Ore.: Multnomah, 2000.

Longaker, Christine. *Facing Death and Finding Hope: A Guide to the Emotional and Spiritual Care of the Dying.* New York: Doubleday, 1997.

Moore, Thomas. *Care of the Soul: A Guide for Cultivating Depth and Sacredness in Everyday Life.* New York: HarperCollins, 1992.

———. *Soul Mates: Honoring the Mysteries of Love and Relationship.* New York: HarperCollins, 1994.

Mother Teresa. *Everything Starts from Prayer.* Edited by Anthony Stern, M.D. Ashland, Ore.: White Cloud Press, 1998.

———. *No Greater Love.* Edited by Becky Benenate and Joseph Durepos. Novato, Calif.: New World Library, 1997.

Ogilvie, Lloyd John. *Why Not? Accept Christ's Healing and Wholeness.* Minneapolis, Minn.: Fleming H. Revell, 1985.

Pipher, Mary. *Another Country: Navigating the Emotional Terrain of Our Elders.* New York: Penguin, 1999.

Pittman, Frank. *Man Enough: Fathers, Sons, and the Search for Masculinity.* New York: Berkeley Publishing Group, 1993.

Pruett, Kyle D. *The Nurturing Father: Journey toward the Complete Man.* New York: Warner Books, 1987.

Schuler, Arvella. *The Positive Family: Possibility Thinking in the Christian Home.* New York: Doubleday, 1982.

Telushkin, Rabbi Joseph. *Jewish Wisdom: Ethical, Spiritual, and Historical Lessons from the Great Works and Thinkers.* New York: William Morrow, 1994.

Wangerin, Jr., Walter. *As for Me and My House: Crafting Your Marriage to Last.* Nashville, Tenn.: Thomas Nelson, 1990.

Wolpe, Rabbi David. *Making Loss Matter: Creating Meaning in Difficult Times.* New York: Putnam, 1999.

INDEX

---

*D*ale Salwak, a professor of English at Southern California's Citrus College, has taught courses and conducted seminars on biblical history and literature for more than twenty-five years. He attended Purdue University (B.A., 1969), which awarded him its Distinguished Alumni Award in 1987, and the University of Southern California (M.A., 1970; Ph.D., 1974) under a National Defense Education Act Fellowship. In 1985 he was awarded a National Endowment for the Humanities grant. Professor Salwak's works include sixteen books on various contemporary literature subjects, as well as *The Wonders of Solitude, The Words of Christ, The Wisdom of Judaism,* and *The Power of Prayer,* all published by New World Library.